A

LATIN VOCABULARY,

ARRANGED ON ETYMOLOGICAL PRINCIPLES,

AS AN

EXERCISE-BOOK

AND

FIRST LATIN DICTIONARY

FOR THE USE OF THE LOWER CLASSES IN SCHOOLS.

BY

BENJAMIN HALL KENNEDY, D.D.

PREBENDARY OF LICHFIELD.

LONDON:

LONGMAN, BROWN, GREEN, AND LONGMANS,
PATERNOSTER ROW.

1848.

PREFACE.

This Latin Vocabulary is designed for the use of beginners, both as Exercise-book and Dictionary. As an Exercise-book, it is to be used after the method suggested, in p. 99, and the ensuing pages, which can be applied to any Latin Grammar. As a Dictionary, it is so arranged that the learner will not only perceive the etymology of the Latin words which he looks out, but will also acquire a knowledge of the derivation of a great number of English words. He will have very little difficulty in finding the words he wants; and what difficulty he has is such as will assist his progress. Most words he will find under their initial letters; attention to the rules here subjoined will direct him to many others; and the few which do not fall under either of these heads he must discover by inquiry from his Master, if they are not indicated in the book he reads.

DIRECTIONS FOR FINDING THE PLACE OF MOST COMPOUNDED WORDS.

Of Compound Words in Latin, the greater number are compounded with Particles, which are the first elements in the Compound. By casting off the Particle, therefore, the second element will appear, under which the word must be sought in the Vocabulary. But as Particles in Composition undergo many changes, a list of these is now given, by attention to which the learner will see what letters to discard.

A (also becomes) ab, abs, (au-fero au-fugio.)
Ad „ „ „ ac, af, ag, al, an, ap, ar, as, at.
Ambi „ „ amb, am, an.
Ante. (anti-cipo.)
Bene.
Circum.
Con „ „ col, com. cor, co, (cog-nosco.)
Contra „ „ contro.
De.

Dis (also becomes) di, dif.

E   „   „   ex, ef.

In   „   „   il, im, ir, (ig-nosco, i-gnarus, i-gnavus.)

Inter   (intel-ligo.)

Intro.

Male.

Ob   „   „   oc, of, og, op, (obs-olesco, os-tendo.)

Per   „   „   pel (pe-ero.)

Præ.

Pro   „   „   prod.

Post.

Præter.

Re   „   „   red.

Retro.

Sub   „   „   suc, suf, sug, sum, sup, sur.

Se   „   „   sed.

Satis.

Subter.

Super.

Sus.

Trans.

Sometimes other inseparable forms commence the Compound, as bi-, tri-, multi-, &c.

The Learner must also remember that

(1) In the Compounds of many words *a* has been changed into *i*, as in those of the following:

> *Ago, cado, cano, frango,*
> *Habeo, lateo, fateor, pango,*
> *Salio, statuo, atque tango;*
> *Capio, rapio, sapio, facio,*
> *Jacio, lacio, placeo, taceo.*

Also in many Compound Adjectives beginning with *in*, as inimicus (in-amicus), irritus (in-ratus).

(2) In the Compounds of many words *a* has been changed into *e*, as in those of the following:

> *Arceo, carpo, damno, lacto,*
> *Fatiscor, fallo, farcio, jacto,*
> *Gradior, patior, partior, tracto,*
> *Pario, patro, atque cando.*
> *Sacro, spargo, atque scando.*

(3) In the Compounds of the following words *a* has been changed into *u* :

  Calco, salto, quatio.

(4) In the Compounds of the following words *e* has been changed into *i* :

  Egeo, teneo, emo,
  Specio, sedeo, premo.

Also in some Compounds of *lego.*

(5) In the Compounds of the following words *æ* has been changed into *i* :

  Quæro, cædo, lædo.

Also in some Adjective Compounds after the Particle *in*, as in-iquus (in-æquus).

(6) Plaudo in Composition becomes -plodo.
 Claudo ,, ,, ,, ,, -cludo.
 Causa ,, ,, ,, ,, -cusa.
 Audio forms obedio.

When, therefore, after casting off the Particle, a form remains which the learner cannot find in the Vocabulary, let him see whether it is one of those which have suffered a Vowel-change; and if so, he must restore its true vowel, and so look it out. Thus, having the word ambigo, and casting off amb, he will change *igo* into *ago*, and look for ambigo under the latter word.

———

ERRATUM.

P. 80, l. 28, for Acbilles read Achilles.

VOCABULARY.

1. A, ab, *from*.
2. abi-es, ĕtis, *fir-tree*.
3. ac, atque, *and*.
4. accipit-er, ris, *hawk*.
5. ac-eo, ĕre, *I am sour*.
6. acerb-us, a, um, *bitter, unripe*.
7. acerv-us, i, *heap*.
8. acu-o, ĕre, *I sharpen*.
9. ad, *to*, AT.
10. adŭl-or, ari, *I flatter*.
1. æd-es, is, *temple*, pl. *house*.
2. æg-er, ra, rum, *sick*.
3. æmul-us, a, um, *rivalling*, EMULOUS.
4. æqu-us, a, um, *level, just*.
5. a-ĕr, ĕris, AIR, *atmosphere*.
6. æ-s, ris, *brass, copper*.
7. æstim-o, are, *I* ESTEEM.
8. æst-us, ūs, *heat, tide*.
9. æst-as, atis, *summer*.
20. æth-ēr, ĕris, *sky*.
1. æv-um, i, *age, time*.
2. ag-er, ri, *field*.
3. agger, is, *mound, rampart* (ad-gero).

5. Acid-us, a, um, ACID. — 8. Acut-us, a, um, *sharpened*, ACUTE. Ac-us, ūs, *needle*. Aci-es, ei, *edge, array, battle*. Ac-er, ris, re, *keen, spirited*: acrimoni-a, æ, ACRIMONY.
10. Adulatio, nis, *flattery*, ADULATION. — 1. Ædil-is, is, *Edile*. Ædific-o, are, *I build* (EDIFY): ædifici-um, i, EDIFICE.—2. Ægrè, *painfully, hardly*. Ægrot-us, a, um, *sick*: ægrot-o, are, *I am sick*.—3. Æmul-or, ari, *I* EMULATE.—4. Æquit-as, atis, EQUITY. Æqu-o, are, *I make even*. Æqual-is, e, EQUAL. Iniqu-us, a, um, *unjust*: iniqnit-as, atis, INIQUITY. Æquor, is, *level surface, sea*.— 7. Existim-o, are, *I deem, I think*.—8. Æstu-o, are, *I boil, chafe* (ESTUARY).
21. Æt-as, atis (for ævitas), *life, age*. Ætern-us, a, um, ETERNAL.—2. Agricol-a, æ, *farmer*: agricultur-a, æ, AGRICULTURE. Perag̈r-o, are, *I traverse*; peregrè, *abroad*; peregrin-us, a, um, *foreign*.—3. Exagger o, are,

A

4. agn-us, i, *lamb*.
5. ag-o, ĕre, *I drive, I do*, (AGENT).
6. ai-o, *I say*, (Def.)
7. al-a, æ, *wing*.
8. alac-er, ris, re, *brisk*.
9. alaud-a, æ, *lark*.
30. alb-us, a, um, *white*.
1. alg-a, æ, *sea-weed*.
2. ali-us, a, ud, *another*.
3. al-o, ĕre, *I nourish*.
4. alter, a, um, *the one, the other*.
5. alt-us, a, um, *high, deep*, (EXALT).
6. alve-us, i, *channel*.
7. amar-us, a, um, *bitter*.
8. amb-o, æ, o, *both*.
9. ambul-o, are, *I walk*, (amb-eo).
40. amict-us, ūs, *clothing* (amicio, ambi-jacio).
1. amic-us, a, um, *friendly*, AMICABLE (amo).
2. amit-a, æ, AUNT.
3. amn-is, is, *river*.
4. am-o, are, *I love*.
5. ampl-us, a, um, *large*, AMPLE.
6. an, *whether? or?*

I pile up, EXAGGERATE.—5. Agil-is, e, *nimble*, AGILE. Agit-o, are, *I ply*, AGITATE. Agm-en, ĭnis, *troop, march*. Act-a, orum, ACTS. Actio, nis, ACTION (ACTIVE). Ambig-o, ere, *I doubt:* ambigu-us, a, um, *doubtful*, AMBIGUOUS. Cog-o, ere, *I gather, compel:* cogit-o, are, *I consider, plan*. Exig-o, ere, *I drive out, levy, finish:* exact-us, a, um, *finished*, EXACT: exigu-us, a, um, *small:* exam-en, ĭnis (for exagimen), *swarm, balance:* examin-o, are, *I weigh*, EXAMINE. Perag-o, ere, *I complete*. Prodig-o, ere, *I lavish;* prodig-us, a, um, *lavish*, PRODIGAL. Redig-o, ere, *I bring back, reduce*. Subig-o, ere, *I subdue*. Transig-o, ere, *I drive through, finish*, TRANSACT.-- 7. Al-es, ĭtis, *winged, bird*.—8. Alacrit-as, atis, *briskness*, ALACRITY.

32. Alien-us, a, um, *strange, averse*, ALIEN.—3. Alm-us, a, um, *bounteous, genial*. Alumn-us, i, *nursling, pupil*. Aliment-um, i, *food*, ALIMENT.—4. Altern-us, a, um, ALTERNATE. Alterc-or, ari, *to dispute with one another*, ALTERCATE.— 5. Altar-e, is, ALTAR.—6. Alvear-e, is, *hive*.

41. Amiciti-a, æ, *friendship*. Inimic-us, a, um, *unfriendly*, ENEMY: inimiciti-æ, arum, ENMITY.—4. Am-or, ŏris, *love* (AMOROUS). Amœn-us, a, um, *pleasant*.

7. an-as, ătis, *duck*.
8. ancill-a, æ, *maid-servant*.
9. ancor-a, æ, ANCHOR.
50.´ ang-o, ĕre, *I pain*.
1. angu-is, is, *snake*.
2. angul-us, i, *corner*, ANGLE.
3. anim-a, æ, *breath, soul*, ANIMATION.
4. anim-us, i, *mind*.
5. ann-us, i, *year*.
6. anser, is, *goose*.
7. ante, *before*.
8. antiqu-us, a, um, ANCIENT, ANTIQUE, (ante).
9. antr-um, i, *cave*.
60. ăn-us, ūs, *old woman*.
1. ap-er, ri, *wild-boar*.
2. ap-ex, ĭcis, *point, tip, peak*.
3. apt-us, a, um, *fit*, APT (apiscor).
4. ap-is, is, *bee*.
5. api-um, i, *parsley*.
6. apric-us, a, um, *sunny*.
7. aqu-a, æ, *water*.
8. aquil-a, æ, EAGLE.
9. aquilo, nis, *north-wind*.
70. ar-a, æ, *altar*.
1. arane-a, æ, *spider*.
2. arbit-er, ri, *umpire*.
3. arbor, is, *tree*.
4. arc-a, æ, *chest*, ARK.
5. arc-eo, ĕre, *I keep off, restrain*.
6. arcess-o, ĕre, *I send for* (ad-cio or accedo).

50. Ang-or, ōris, *pain*, ANGUISH. Angust-us, a, um, *narrow*. Anxi-us, a, um, ANXIOUS.—1. Anguill-a, æ, *eel*.—3. Animal, is, ANIMAL. Inanim-us, a, um, *lifeless*, INANIMATE.—4. Animadvert-o, ere, *I attend, remark, punish* (ANIMAD-VERSION). Unanim-is, e (us, a, um), UNANIMOUS.—5. Annu-us, a, um, ANNUAL. Annal-es, ium, ANNALS. Annon-a, æ, *yearly produce, yearly price of corn* (ANNI-VERSARY).—7. Antiquit-as, atis, ANTIQUITY.
63. Apt-o, are, *I* ADAPT. Adipisc-or, i, *I obtain* (ADEPT). Inept-us, a, um, *inapt, silly*.
72. Arbitri-um, i, *decision*, ARBITRATION, *will*. Arbitr-or, ari, *I* ARBITRATE, *judge, think*.—4. Arcan-us, a, um, *secret*.—5. Arct-us, a, um, *confined*. Coerc-eo, ĕre, *I confine, constrain* (COERCION). Exerc-eo, ĕre, I EXERCISE:

4

7. arc-us, ŭs, *bow*, ARCH.
8. ard-eo, ēre, *I am on fire*, (ARDENT).
9. ardu-us, a, um, *steep, lofty*, ARDUOUS.
80. aren-a, æ, *sand.*
1. arid-us, a, um, *dry* (areo).
2. argent-um, i, *silver.*
3. argill-a, æ, *clay.*
4. argu-o, ēre, *I prove*, ARGUE.
5. ari-es, ĕtis, *ram.*
6. arist-a, æ, *ear of corn.*
7. arm-a, orum, ARMS, ARMOUR, (Def.)
8. ar-o, are, *I plough* (ARABLE).
9. ar-s, tis, ART.
90. art-us, uum, *limbs*, (Def.)
1. arund-o, ĭnis, *reed.*
2. ar-x, cis, *citadel* (arceo).
3. as, sis, *a coin and weight.*
4. asin-us, i, ASS.
5. asper, a, um, *rough.*
6. ass-us, a, um, *roasted.*
7. astr-um, i, *star* (ASTRONOMY).
8. ast, at, *but.*
9. ast-us, ŭs, *craft.*
100. at-er, ra, rum, *black.*
1. atri-um, i, *court yard, hall.*
2. atr-ox, ocis, *cruel*, ATROCIOUS.
3. aud-eo, ēre, *I dare.*
4. aud-io, ire, *I hear.*
5. avar-us, a, um, *covetous*, AVARICIOUS (aveo).
6. aven-a, æ, *oat.*
7. av-eo, ēre, *I covet.*

exercit-us, ŭs, *army.*—8. Ard-or, oris, *heat*, ARDOUR.
84. Argument-um, i, *proof*, ARGUMENT.—7. Arm-o, are, I ARM (ARMAMENT). Inerm-is, e, *unarmed.*—8. Aratrum, i, *plough.* Arv-um, i, *field.* Arment-um, i, *herd.*— 9. Artif-ex, ĭcis, ARTIFICER; artifici-um, i, *skill, trade,* ARTIFICE. Iner-s, tis, *skilless, inactive,* INERT.
90. Articul-us, i, *joint,* ARTICLE.—5. Exasper-o, are, *I roughen,* EXASPERATE.—9. Astut-us, a, um, *crafty.*
100. Atrament-um, i, *ink.*—3. Aud-ax, acis, *daring,* AUDACIOUS.—4. Audienti-a, æ, *hearing,* AUDIENCE. Obed-io, ire, I OBEY (OBEDIENT).—5. Avariti-a, æ, AVARICE.— 7. Avid-us, a, um, *greedy;* avidit-as, atis, *greediness,*

8. aug-eo, ēre, *I increase*, AUGMENT.
9. av-is is, *bird*, (AVIARY).
110. augur, is, *soothsayer*, AUGUR, (avis).
  1. aul-a, æ, HALL.
  2. aur-a, æ, *breeze*.
  3. aur-is, is, EAR.
  4. àurig-a, æ, *charioteer*.
  5. auror-a, æ, *morning*.
  6. aur-um, i, *gold*.
  7. auscult-o, are, *I listen*.
  8. aust-er, ri, *south-wind*.
  9. autem, *but*.
120. auster-us, a, um, *dry*, AUSTERE.
  1. autumn-us, i, AUTUMN (augeo).
  2. av-us, i, *grandfather*.
  3. auxili-um, i, *help*, (AUXILIARY), (augeo).
  4. ax-is, is, AXLE, *pole*.
  5. Bacc-a, æ, *berry*.
  6. bacul-us, i, *staff*.
  7. balb-us, a, um, *stammering*.
  8. balne-um, i, (private) BATH : balne-æ, arum, (public) *baths*.
  9. bal-o, are, *I BLEAT*.
130. barb-a, æ, BEARD.
  1. barbar-us, a, um, BARBAROUS.
  2. basi-um, i, *kiss*, BUSS.
  3. beat-us, a, um, *blessed* (beo).
  4. bellu-a, æ, *monster*.
  5. bell-um, i, *war*.
  6. bell-us, a, um, *pretty* (bonus).
  7. besti-a, æ, BEAST.

AVIDITY.—8. Auctio, nis, AUCTION. Auct-or, ōris, *adviser, promoter, informer*, AUTHOR. Auctorit-as, atis, *influence, recommendation*, AUTHORITY.—9. Auc-eps, upis (for aviceps), *fowler;* aucup-or, ari, *I catch, lie in wait for*.
110. Ausp-ex, icis (for avispex), *soothsayer:* auspici-um, i, AUSPICE. Augur-or, ari, *I divine:* august-us, a, um, *sacred*, AUGUST.
121. Avi-a, æ, *grandmother*. Avuncul-us, i, UNCLE.—6. Imbecill-us, a, um, *weak*, IMBECILE.—6. Balbut-io, ire, *I stammer*.
134. Bell-o, are, *I make war;* debell-o, are, *I conquer;* rebell-o, are, I REBEL: rebell-is, e, REBEL; rebellio, nis, REBELLION.—7. Imbib-o, ere, *I* IMBIBE (wine-BIB-
A3

8. bib-o, ĕre, *I drink*.
9. bil-is, is, BILE.
140. bland-us, a, um, *soothing*, BLAND.
1. bon-us, a, um, *good*.
2. bo-a, vis, *ox*.
3. brachi-um, i, *lower part of the arm*.
4. brev-is, e, *short*, BRIEF.
5. brum-a, æ, *mid-winter*.
6. brut-us, a, um, *irrational*, BRUTE.
7. bubo, nis, *owl*.
8. Cacum-en, inis, *tip, top*.
9. cad-o, ĕre, *I fall*.
150. cad-us, i, *cask*.
1. cæc-us, a, um, *blind*.
2. cæd-o, ĕre, *I cut, beat, kill*.
3. cæl-ebs, ibis, (Adj.) *unmarried*, (CELIBACY).
4. cæremoni-a, a, CEREMONY.
5. cærule-us, a, um, *azure*.
6. calam-us, i, *stalk, reed*.
7. calamit-as, atis, CALAMITY, (calamus).
8. calath-us, i, *basket*.
9. calendæ, arum, *calends*, (pl.)
160. caleo, ēre, *I am warm*.
1. calig-o, inis, *darkness*.

BER).—9. Bland-ior, iri, *I flatter, soothe*; blandiment-um, i, BLANDISHMENT.

140. Bonit-as, atis, *goodness*, BOUNTY. Bene, *well*: benign-us, a, um, *kind*, BENIGN.—2. Boo, are, *I bellow*: rebo-o, are, *I rebellow, echo*. Bubulc-us, i, *cowherd*.—9. Caduc-us, a, um, *frail, dropping*. Cadaver, is, *corpse*, (CADAVEROUS). Cas-us, ūs, *chance*, CASE, (CASUAL). Accid-o, ĕre, *I fall towards*: accidit, *it happens*, (ACCIDENT.) Incid-o, ĕre, *I fall in* or *upon*: incidit, *it befalls*, (INCIDENT). Occid-o, ĕre, *I fall down, die, set*: occas-us, us, *setting, fall*: occasio, nis, *opportunity*, OCCASION. Also, oon, de, ex, inter, pro, re,-cido.

151. Cæc-o, ex, ob,-cæc-o, are, *I blind*.—2. Cæd-es, is, *murder, slaughter*. Cæment-um, i, *hewn stone*, (CEMENT). Cæsari-es, ei, *hair*. Decid-o, ĕre, *I cut down, settle*, DECIDE: decisio, nis, DECISION. Incid-o, ĕre, *I cut in* or *on*, (INCISION). Occid-o, ere, *I kill*. Also, abs, ac, circum, con, ex, præ, re, suc,-cido.

160. Cal-or, ŏris, *heat*: calid-us, a, um, *hot*.—7. Calce-us, i, *shoe*.

2. calix, ĭcis, *cup*, CHALICE.
3. call-is, is, *path*.
4. callid-us, a, um, *crafty*.
5. calumni-a, a, CALUMNY.
6. calv-us, a, um, *bald*.
7. cal-x, cis, *heel*, CHALK.
8. camel-us, i, CAMEL.
9. camer-a, æ, CHAMBER.
170. camin-us, i, CHIMNEY, *oven*.
1. camen-a, æ, *muse*, (cano).
2. camp-us, i, *plain*, *field*.
3. canal-is, is, CANAL.
4. canc-er, ri, *crab*.
5. cand-eo, ēre, *I am white*.
6. can-is, is, *dog*.
7. cann-a, æ, CANE.
8. can-o, ĕre, *I sing*.
9. can-us, a, um, *hoary*.
180. cap-er, ri, *he-goat*.
1. capill-us, i, *hair*, (caput).
2. cap-io, ĕre, *I take*, (CAPTURE.)
3. cap-ut, itis, *head*.
4. carb-o, onis, *coal*.
5. carcer, is, *prison*.

Calc-ar, aris, *spur*. Calc-o, are, *I trample* : con, in, pro,-culco, are, (INCULCATE).
175. Cand-or, ōris, *whiteness*, CANDOUR. Candid-us, a, um, *white*, CANDID. Candidat-us, i, *clad in white*, CANDIDATE. Candel-a, æ, CANDLE. Accend-o, ĕre, *I light up*: incend-o, ĕre, *I inflame*, (INCENSED, INCENDIARY).—6. Catul-us, i, *puppy*, *whelp*.—8. Canor-us, a, um, *tuneful*. Cant-us, us, *song*, CHANT. Cant-o, are, *I sing*. Also, ac, con, præ, suc,-cino, ĕre, (ACCENT).—9. Caniti-es, ei, *white hair*, *hoariness*. Can-eo, ĕre, *I am hoary*.
182. Cap-ax, acis, CAPACIOUS. Captiv-us, a, um, CAPTIVE. Capt-o, are, *I catch at*. Capess-o, ere, *I undertake*. Accip-io, ĕre, *I receive*, ACCEPT. Concip-io, ĕre, I CONCEIVE. Decip-io, ĕre, I DECEIVE, (DECEPTION), Excip-io, ere, I EXCEPT. Incip-io, ĕre, *I begin*. Percip-io, ĕre, I PERCEIVE, *acquire*. Præcip-io, ĕre, *I forestall*, *direct*: præcept-um, i, PRECEPT. Recip-io, ĕre, *I take back*, RECEIVE, (RECEPTACLE). Suscip-io, ere, *I undertake*. —3. Capital-is, e, CAPITAL. Anc-eps, ipitis, *double-faced*, *doubtful*. Præc-eps, ipitis, *headlong*, (PRECIPICE).

6. card-o, inis, *hinge*, (CARDINAL).
7. car-eo, ēre, *I am without.*
8. carin-a, æ, *keel, ship.*
9. carm-en, inis, *verse, poem.*
190. car-o, nis, *flesh,* (CARNAL).
1. carp-o, ĕre, *I crop, pluck.*
2. car-us, a, um, *dear.*
3. cas-a, æ, *cottage.*
4. case-us, i, CHEESE.
5. castr-um, i, *fort,* Pl. *camp.*
6. cast-us, a, um, CHASTE.
7. caten-a, æ, CHAIN.
8. caterv-a, æ, *crowd, troop.*
9. caud-a, æ, *tail.*
200. cav-eo, ēre, *I beware.*
1. caul-a, æ, *sheepcote.*
2. caul-is, is, *stalk.*
3. caupo, nis, *innkeeper.*
4. caus-a, æ, CAUSE.
5. cav-us, a, um, *hollow,* (CAVE, CAVITY).
6. ced-o, ĕre, *I yield,* CEDE, *go.*
7. cedr-us, i, CEDAR-*tree.*
8. celeb-er, ris, re, *famous,* (CELEBRITY).
9. celer, is, e, *swift,* (CELERITY).

191. Decerp-o, ere, *I pluck off.* Also, con, dis, ex,-cerpo.—
6. Castig-o, are, 1 CHASTISE. Incest-us, a, um, *impure.*
200. Caut-us, a, um, *guarded,* CAUTIOUS. Cautio, nis,
CAUTION.—4. Accus-o, are, I ACCUSE. Excus-o, are,
I EXCUSE. Recus-o, are, I REFUSE.—5. Cavern-a, æ,
CAVERN.—6. Cessio, nis, CESSION. Cess-o, are, I
CEASE, *loiter.* Acced-o, ere, *I approach,* ACCEDE, *am
added,* (ACCESSION). Anteced-o, ere, *I go before,* (ANTE-
CEDENT, ANCESTOR). Conced-o, ere, *I yield,* CONCEDE,
(CONCESSION). Deced-o, ere, *I depart from,* (DECEASE).
Disced-o, ere, *I depart.* Exced-o, ere, *I go out from,*
EXCEED, (EXCESS). Inced-o, ere, *I step on, advance.*
Interced-o, ere, *I go between,* INTERCEDE. Præced-o, ere,
I go before, PRECEDE. Proced-o, ere, *I go forward,*
PROCEED, (PROCEEDING, PROCESSION). Reced-o,
ere, *I go back,* RECEDE. Seced-o, ere, *I go apart,*
SECEDE. Succed-o, ere, *I go under, come up to,*
SUCCEED, (SUCCESS, SUCCESSOR).—8. Celebr-o,
are, *I frequent,* CELEBRATE.—9. Celer-o, are; acceler-o,
are, *I hasten,* ACCELERATE.

210. cell-a, æ, *vault*, CELL, CELLAR.
  1. cell-o, ĕre, *I move*, (obs.)
  2. cel-o, are, *I* CONCEAL.
  3. cels-us, a, um, *high.*
  4. cens-eo, ēre, *I think, judge,* CENSURE.
  5. centum, *hundred.*
  6. cer-a, æ, *wax.*
  7. ceras-us, i, CHERRY-*tree.*
  8. cern-o, ĕre, *divide, perceive.*
  9. cert-us, a, um, CERTAIN, (cerno).
220. cert-o, are, *I vie, contend.* (cerno).
  1. cerv-ix, īcis, *neck.*
  2. cerv-us, i, *stag.*
  3. cesp-es, ĭtis, *turf.*
  4. ceter-us, a, um, *the rest.*
  5. ceu, *as.*
  6. chart-a, æ, *paper,* CHART.
  7. chord-a, æ, *string,* CHORD.
  8. chorus, i, CHOIR, *dance.*
  9. cib-us, i, *food.*
230. cicad-a, æ, *grasshopper.*
  1. ciconi-a, æ, *stork.*
  2. cicut-a, æ, *hemlock.*
  3. ci-eo, ēre, } *I stir up.*
    c-io, īre, }
  4. cili-um, i, *eye-brow*, (obs.)
  5. cing-o, ĕre, *I surround, gird.*

210. Excell-o, ĕre, I EXCEL; also, præ, ante,-cello. Percell-o, ere, *I strike, thrill.*—4. Cens-or, oris, CENSOR. Cens-us, ûs, *taxing, tax-roll.* Recens-eo, ere, *I review.* Succens-eo, ere, *I am secretly angry with.*—5. Centuri-a, æ, *a body of* 100, (CENTURY, CENTURION).—8. Decern-o, ere, I DECREE; decret-um, i, DECREE. Discern-o, ere, *I distinguish,* DISCERN: discrim-en, inis, *difference, danger,* (DISCRIMINATE, DISCREET). Secern-o, ere, *I separate;* secret-us, a, um, SECRET.
220. Certam-en, inis, *contest.*—8. Chore-a, æ, *dance.*
233. Cit-us, a, um, *swift.* Cit-o, are, *I proclaim,* CITE: recit-o, are, I RECITE: suscit-o, are, *I rouse:* concit-o, are, *I excite:* conci-o, nis, *popular assembly, harangue:* excit-o, are, I EXCITE: incit-o, are, I INCITE.—4. Concili-um, i, *gathering,* COUNCIL: concili-o, are, *I draw together,* CON-CILIATE: reconcili-o, are, I RECONCILE. Supercili-um, i, *brow, arrogance,* (SUPERCILIOUS).—5. Also, ac, in,

6. cin-is, eris, *ashes.*
7. circ-us, i, CIRCLE, CIRCUS.
8. cithar-a, æ, *harp,* GUITAR.
9. cis, *this side of.*
240. civ-is, is, *citizen.*
1. clad-es, is, *ruin, defeat.*
2. clam, *secretly.*
3. clam-o, are, *I cry out,* (CLAIM).
4. clar-us, a, um, CLEAR, *bright, illustrious.*
5. class-is, is, *a fleet,* (CLASS, CLASSIC).
6. clav-a, æ, CLUB.
7. claud-us, a, um, *lame.*
8. clav-is, is, *key.*
9. clav-us, i, *nail.*
250. clemen-s, tis, (adj.) *merciful.*
1. clien-s, tis, CLIENT.
2. clin-o, are, *I lean,* (obs.)
3. clype-us, i, *shield.*
4. cœl-um, i, *heaven.*
5. cœn-a, æ, *supper, dinner.*
6. cœn-um, i, *mud.*

præ, suc,-cingo. (PRECINCT, SUCCINCT).—7. Circa, circum, circiter, *around, about.* Circul-or, ari, *I gad,* CIRCULATE. Idcirco, *therefore.*—9. Citra, *this side of :* citeri-or, oris, *inner, nearer.*

240. Civit-as, atis, CITY, *state.* Civil-is, e, *belonging to the city,* CIVIL.—2. Clandestin-us, a, um, *secret,* CLANDESTINE. 3. Clam-or, oris, *shout,* CLAMOUR. Acclam-o, are, *I shout at,* (ACCLAMATION). Declam-o, are, I DECLAIM. Exclam-o, are, *I cry out,* EXCLAIM, (EXCLAMATION). Proclam-o, are, I PROCLAIM, (PROCLAMATION). Also, con, in, re, suc,-clamo.—4. Præclar-us, a, um, *illustrious.* Declar-o, are, I DECLARE.—7. Claudic-o, are, *I limp.*— 8. Claud-o, ere, *I shut,* (CLAUSE): claustr-um, i, *barrier:* conclud-o, ere, *I shut up,* CONCLUDE, (CONCLUSION): ex, in, præ, se,-cludo, I EX—IN—PRE–SE—CLUDE.

250. Clementi-a, æ, CLEMENCY. Inclemen-s, tis, *unkind,* INCLEMENT.—2. Cliv-us, i, *hill,* CLIFF: accliv-is, e, *sloping upward,* (ACCLIVITY): decliv-is, e, *sloping downward,* (DECLIVITY): procliv-is, e, *sloping forward, easy, inclined.* Acclin-o, are, *I lean on.* Declin-o, are, *I lean from,* DECLINE, (DECLENSION), Inclin-o, are, *I lean towards,* INCLINE, (INCLINATION). Reclin-o, are, *I lean back,* RECLINE.—4. Cœlest-is, e, *heavenly,* CELESTIAL.—5. Cœno, are, *I sup, dine.*

7. cœp-i, isse, *I begin*, (Def.)
8. cohor-s, tis, COHORT.
9. coll-is, is, *hill.*
260. coll-um, i, *neck.*
  1. col-o, ĕre, *I till, worship.*
  2. col-or, ōris, COLOUR.
  3. columb-a, æ, *pigeon.*
  4. col-us, i, *distaff.*
  5. com-a, æ, *hair, leaf.*
  6. com-es, itis, *companion,* (cum-eo).
  7. com-is, is, *affable.*
  8. com-o, ĕre, *I adorn,* COMB.
  9. comœdi-a, æ, COMEDY.
270. compit-a, orum, *cross roads.*
  1. conch-a, æ, *shell.*
  2. cond-io, ire, *I season.*
  3. con-or, ari, *I endeavour.*
  4. consul-o, ere, I CONSULT.
  5. contra, *against.*
  6. copi-a, æ, *plenty,* pl. *troops,* (COPIOUS) (co-ops).
  7. copul-a, æ, *tie.*
  8. coqu-o, ere, I COOK.
  9. cor, dis, *heart,* (CORDIAL).
280. coram, *in presence.*
  1. corb-is, is, *basket.*
  2. cori-um, i, *hide, leather.*
  3. corn-ix, icis, *crow.*
  4. corn-u, u, HORN.
  5. coron-a, æ, CROWN, *garland.*
  6. corp-us, ŏris, *body,* (CORPSE, CORPORAL).
  7. cort-ex, ïcis, *bark.*
  8. corusc-us, a, um, *glittering.*

261 Colon-us, i, *tiller, settler;* coloni-a, æ, COLONY. Cult-or, oris, CULTIVATER, *worshipper.* Cultur-a, æ, *tillage,* CULTURE: cult-us, us, CULTIVATION, *worship.* Incol-o, ere, *I inhabit;* incol-a, æ, *inhabitant.* Also, ac, circum, re, -colo.—5. Comet-es, or Comet-a, æ, COMET.—6. Comit-or, ari, *I accompany.*—9. Comic-us, a, um, COMIC.
274 Consul, is, CONSUL. Consili-um, i, COUNSEL.—5 Contrari-us, a, um, CONTRARY.—7. Copul-o, are, *I unite,* COUPLE.—9. Concor-s, dis, *agreeing;* concord-ia, æ, CONCORD. Discor-s, dis, *disagreeing;* discordi-a, æ, DISCORD. Record-or, ari, *I remember,* (RECORD). Socor-s, dis, *stupid.*

9. corv-us, i, *raven.*
290. cō-s, tis, *whetstone.*
  1. cothurn-us, i, *buskin.*
  2. coturn-ix, īcis, *quail.*
  3. cras, *to-morrow.*
  4. crass-us, a, um, *thick,* COARSE.
  5. cratēr, is, *bowl.*
  6. creb-er, ra, rum, *frequent.*
  7. cred-o, ĕre, *I believe, trust,* (CREED).
  8. cre-o, are, I CREATE, (CREATION).
  9. crep-o, are, *I patter.*
300. cresc-o, ere, *I grow.*
  1. cret-a, æ, *chalk.*
  2. cribr-um, i, *sieve,* (cerno).
  3. crim-en, inis, *charge,* CRIME, (cerno).
  4. crin-is, is, *hair,* (cerno).
  5. crisp-us, a, um, *curly.*
  6. crist-a, æ, CREST.
  7. croc-us, i, *saffron.*
  8. crud-us, a, um, *raw,* CRUDE, (cruor).
  9. crumen-a, æ, *purse.*
310. cru-or, oris, *blood.*
  1. cru-s, ris, *leg.*
  2. cru-x, cis, CROSS.
  3. cub-o, are, *I lie down.*
  4. cud-o, ĕre, *I fabricate.*
  5. cul-ex, īcis, *gnat.*
  6. culin-a, æ, *kitchen.*
  7. culm-en, inis, *summit.*
  8. culp-a, æ, *fault.*

297. Credul-us, a, um, *trusting,* CREDULOUS. Credibil-is, e, CREDIBLE. Credit-or, oris, CREDITOR.—8. Recre-o, are, *I refresh,* (RECREATION).—9. Crepundi-a, orum, *rattles, toys.* Discrep-o, are, *I differ.* Increp-o, are, *I chide.*
300. Decresc-o, ere, I DECREASE. Incresc-o, ere, I INCREASE. —8. Crudel-is, e, CRUEL.
310. Cruent-us, a, um, *bloody.*—2. Cruci-o, discruci-o, excruci-o, are, *I torture,* EXCRUCIATE.— 3. Cubit-us, i, *elbow,* CUBIT. Cubil-e, is, *bed-chamber.* Excub-o, are, *I watch, lie awake.* Incub-o, are, *I lie on, brood.* Recub-o, are, *I recline.* Also, ac, oc,-cubo. Incumb-o, ere, *I lean on, apply to,* (INCUMBENT). Recumb-o, ere, *I recline, fall back,* (RECUMBENT). Also, ac, dis, oc, pro, suc,-cumbo. —8. Culp-o, are, *I blame,* (CULPABLE).

9. cult-er, ri, *knife.*
320. cum, *with.*
  1. cumul-us, i, *heap.*
  2. cun-æ, arum, *cradle.*
  3. cunct-us, a, um, *all together,* (cŭnque).
  4. cunque, *all-soever.*
  5. cup-io, ĕre, *I desire.*
  6. cupress-us, i, CYPRESS-tree.
  7. cur, *why ?*
  8. cur-a, æ, CARE.
  9. curi-a, æ, *senate-house.*
330. curr-o, ĕre, *I run.*
  1. curv-us, a, um, *crooked, winding,* (CURVE.)
  2. cusp-is, idis, *point* (of weapon.)
  3. cust-os, ōdis, *guardian.*
  4. cut-is, is, *skin.*
  5. cyath-us, i, *cup.*
  6. cycn-us, i, *swan,* (CYGNET).
  7. cymb-a, æ, *boat.*
  8. Dam-a, æ, *deer.*
  9. damn-um, i, *loss,* DAMAGE.
340. (daps) dap-is, *banquet,* (Def.)
  1. de, *from, concerning.*
  2. deb-eo, ēre, *I owe,* (de-habeo).
  3. debil-is, e, *weak,* (de-habeo), (DEBILITY).
  4. decem, *ten,* (Num.)
  5. dec-et, ēre, *it beseemeth,* (Impers.)
  6. del-eo, ēre, *I blot out,* (leo) (INDELIBLE).

321. Cumul-o, accumul-o, are, *I heap,* ACCUMULATE. 5. Cupid-us, a, um, *desirous:* cupid-o, inis, *desire,* CUPID. 8. Cur-o, are, *I take care of.* Accurat-us, a, um, ACCURATE. Procur-o, are, *I care for,* PROCURE. Secur-us, a, um, *careless,* SECURE. Curios-us, a, um, *careful,* CURIOUS.
330. Curr-us, ŭs, *chariot.* Curs-us, ŭs, *race,* COURSE. Con, de, dis, ex, in, oc, per, præ, pro, re,-curro. (CONCOURSE, DIS-COURSE, EXCURSION, INCUR, OCCUR, RECUR, &c.) Succurr-o, *I help,* SUCCOUR. — 3. Custodi-a, æ, *guard,* CUSTODY.—9. Damn-o, condemn-o, are, I CONDEMN.
341. Dein, deinde, *then, next.* Deinceps, *next in order.*—2. Debit-um, i, DEBT. Debit-r, oris, DEBTOR.—5. Decen-s, tis, *becoming,* DECENT. Dec-or, ōris, *elegance:* decor-us, a, um, *elegant, honourable,* DECOROUS. Dec-us, ōris, *honour.* Decŏr-o, are, *I adorn,* DECORATE. Dedec-us, ōris, *disgrace.*

B

7. dem-o, ĕre, *I take away*, (de-emo).
8. demum, *at last*.
9. denique, *finally*.
350. den-s, tis, *tooth*, (DENTIST).
1. dens-us, a, um, *thick, close*, DENSE.
2. de-us, i, *God*, DEITY.
3. dexter, a, um, *right, (not left)* DEXTEROUS.
4. diadema, tis, DIADEM.
5. dīc-o, ĕre, *I say*.
6. dĭc-o, are, *I devote*.
7. di-es, ei, DAY.
8. digit-us, i, *finger*.
9. dign-us, a, um, *worthy*.
360. dir-us, a, um, *accursed, dreadful*, DIRE.
1. disc-o, ĕre, *I learn*.
2. div-es, ĭtis, (Adj.) *rich*.
3. do, dăre, *I give*, (DATE).
4. doc-eo, ēre, *I teach*.

352. Div-us, i, *deity*: divin-us, a, um, DIVINE.—5. Dict-um, i, *a saying*. Dictio, nis, *saying*, DICTION. Dict-o, are, I DICTATE, (DICTATOR). Benedic-o, ere, *I bless*, (BENEDICTION). Edic-o, ere, *I order*, (EDICT). Prædic-o, ere, *I foretell*, (PREDICTION). Also, ad, con, contra, in, inter, male,-dico, (CONTRADICT).—6. Abdic-o, are, I ABDICATE. Dedic-o, are, I DEDICATE. Indic-o, are, *I inform*, INDICATE: ind-ex, icis, *informer*: indici-um, i, *token, information*. Prædic-o, are, *I proclaim*, PREACH. —7. Diu, *long*: diuturn-us, a, um, *long-lasting*. Diurn-us, a, um, *daily*. Diari-um, i, DIARY. Hodie, *to-day*. Meridi-es, ei, *noon*. Perendie, *the day after to-morrow*. Postridie, *the day after*. Pridie, *the day before*. Quotidie, *daily*.—9. Dignit-as, atis, *worth*, DIGNITY. Dign-or, ari, *I deem worthy*, DEIGN: dedign-or, ari, I DISDAIN. Indign-us, a, um, *unworthy*, (INDIGNITY): indign-or, ari, *I deem unworthy*, (INDIGNANT, INDIGNATION).
360. Dir-æ, arum, *curses, furies*. — 1. Discipul-us, i, *scholar*, DISCIPLE: disciplin-a, æ, *teaching*, DISCIPLINE, *sect*. Dedisc-o, ere, *I unlearn*. Also, ad, con, e, per,-disco.— 2. Diviti-æ, arum, *riches*. Dit-o, are, *I enrich*. Ditesc-o, ere, *I grow rich*.—3. Add-o, ere, I ADD. Cond-o, ere, *I hide, found*. Ded-o, ere, *I surrender*. Ed-o, ere, *I give out, publish*, EDIT. Perd-o, ere, *I lose*, (PERDITION). Prod-o, ere, *I betray*. Redd-o, ere, *I restore*. Trad-o, ere, *I deliver*, (TRADITION).—4. Document-um, i, *proof*, DOCUMENT. Docil-is, e. *teachable*, DOCILE. Doct-us, a, um, *learned*. Doct-or, oris, *teacher*, DOCTOR. Dedoc-eo, ere, *I unteach*.

5. dol-eo, ēre, *I grieve, I feel pain.*
6. dol-us, ì, *deceit.*
7. domin-us, i, *lord,* (domus).
8. dom-o, are, *I tame.*
9. dom-us, us, *house,* (DOME).
370. donec, *until.*
  1. don-o, are, *I present,* (do).
  2. dorm-io, ire, *I sleep.*
  3. dors-um, i, *back.*
  4. dos, dotis, DOWRY, (do).
  5. draco, nis, DRAGON.
  6. dubi-us, a, um, DOUBTFUL, (duo).
  7. duc-o, ĕre, *I lead.*
  8. dulc-is, e, *sweet.*
  9. duell-um, i, *war, battle,* (DUEL).
380. dum, *whilst, until.*
  1. dum-us, i, *thicket.*
  2. duo, æ, o, TWO.
  3. duo, ere, *I put on,* (obs.)
  4. durus, a, um, *hard.*
  5. Ebri-us, a, um, *drunken.*
  6. eb-ur, ŏris, IVORY.
  7. ecce, en, *lo!*
  8. ĕd-o, ere, I EAT, (irreg.)
  9. eg-eo, ēre, *I need.*

Doctrin-a, æ, *teaching,* DOCTRINE. Also, ad, con, e, per, -doceo.— 5. Dol-or, oris, *pain, grief.*—6. Dolos-us, a, um, *deceitful.*—7. Domin-or, ari, *I rule,* (DOMINION).— 8. Indomit-us, a, um, *untamed.*—9. Domestic-us, a, um, DOMESTIC.

371. Don-um, i, *gift,* DONATION.—6. Dubit-o, are, I DOUBT. —7. Du-x, cis, *leader,* (DUKE). Ab, ad, circum, con, de, di, e, in, intro, ob, per, præ, pro, re, se, sub, tra,-duco, (ABDUCTION, ADDUCE, CONDUCE, CONDUCT, DEDUCE, INDUCE, INTRODUCE, PRODUCE, REDUCE, &c.) Edŭc-o, are, I EDUCATE.—8. Dulced-o, inis, *sweetness.*

381. Dumtaxat, *only, at least.*—2. Dupl-ex, icis, DOUBLE.— 3. Indu-o, ere, *I put on.* Exu-o, ere, *I put off.* Exuvi-æ, *strippings, spoils.*—4. Dur-o, are, *I harden, last,* ENDURE, (OBDURATE).—5. Ebriet-as, atis, *drunkenness,* EBRIETY. —8. Ed-ax, acis, *devouring.* Esur-io, ire, *I am hungry.*— 9. Egest-as, atis, *want.* Indig-eo, ere, *I am in want,* (INDIGENT).

390. ejul-o, are, *I howl.*
1. elegan-s, tis, (Adj.) ELEGANT, (eligo.)
2. element-um, i, ELEMENT.
3. em-o, ere, *I buy, take.*
4. enim, *for.*
5. ens-is, is, *sword.*
6. eo, ire, *I go,* (irreg.)
7. epistol-a, æ, *letter,* EPISTLE.
8. epul-æ, arum, *banquet.* (edo).
9. equ-us, i, *horse.*
400. erga, *towards.*
1. ergo, *therefore.*
2. err-o, are, *I wander,* ERR.
3. esc-a, æ, *food,* (edo).
4. essed-um, i, *car, waggon.*
5. et, *and.*
6. ex, e, *out of, from.*
7. exempl-um, i, EXAMPLE, (eximo).
8. exta, orum, *entrails.*
9. extra, *outside of.*
410. Fab-a, æ, *bean.*

393. Adim-o, ere; dem-o. ere, *I take away.* Dirim-o, ere, *I separate, terminate.* Exim-o, ere, *I take out,* EXEMPT : Eximi-us, a, um, *choice, eminent.* Interim-o, ere; perim-o, ere, *I destroy.* Redim-o, ere, I REDEEM, (REDEMPTION). —6. It-er, ineris, *journey,* (ITINERANT). Abeo, *I go away.* Adeo, *I go to, approach :* adit-us, us, *approach.* Ambio, *I go round, canvass :* ambitio, nis, *canvassing, intrigue,* AMBITION : ambitios-us, a, um, AMBITIOUS. Circumeo, *I go around :* circuit-us, us, CIRCUIT. Coeo, *I meet, assemble :* cœt-us, us, *meeting.* Exeo, *I go out :* exit-us, us, *going out,* EXIT : exiti-um, i, *destruction.* Ineo, *I go in, enter, begin :* initi-um, i, *beginning.* Intereo, *I sink, die :* interit-us, us, *fall, death.* Obeo, *I visit, traverse, undergo, die :* obit-us, us, *departure, death.* Pereo, I PERISH. Præeo, *I go before.* Prætereo, *I pass by.* Prodeo, *I go forth.* Redeo, *I go back, return :* redit-us, us, *return.* Subeo, *I go under, enter, undergo :* subit-us, a, um, SUDDEN. Transeo, *I go over, cross, pass :* transit-us, us, *passage,* (TRANSITION, TRANSITORY). Seditio, nis, *going apart,* SEDITION.— 9. Equ-es, itis, *horseman, knight.* Equit-o, are, *I ride :* equitat-us, us, *cavalry.*
402. Err-or, oris, *wandering,* ERROUR. Ab, ob, per,-erro.— 5 Etiam, *also.* Etsi, *although.*—7. Exempl-ar, áris, *pattern,* SAMPLE, (EXEMPLARY).

1. fab-er, ri, *smith, carpenter.*
2. fabul-a, æ, *story, play,* FABLE, (fari).
3. facet-us, a, um, *witty, quick-tongued.*
4. faci-es, ei, FACE, (facio).
5. fac-io, ĕre, *I do, make.*
6. facund-us, a, um, *eloquent,* (fari).
7. fæ-x, cis, *dregs.*
8. fag-us, i, *beech-tree.*
9. fall-o, ĕre, *I deceive.*
420. fal-x, cis, *hook, sickle.*
1. fam-a, æ, *report,* FAME, (fari).
2. fam-es, is, *hunger,* FAMINE.
3. famul-us, i, *servant.*
4. fan-um, i, *shrine. temple,* FANE.
5. far, ris, *bread-corn.*
6. farc-io, ire, *I stuff.*
7. fas, *right,* (fari).

411. Fabric-a, æ, FABRIC: fabric-o, are, *I fashion,* FABRI-
CATE.—2. Fabulos-us, a, um, FABULOUS.—3. Faceti-æ,
arum, *wit,* (FACETIOUS).—5. Facil-is, e, *easy:* facult-as,
atis, *power,* FACULTY: difficil-is, e, DIFFICULT:
difficult-as, atis, DIFFICULTY. Facin-us, oris, *deed, crime.*
Fact-um, i, *deed,* FACT. Factio, nis, *making,* FACTION.
Affic-io, ere, I AFFECT, *visit.* Benefaci-o, ere, *I do good to:*
benefici-um, i, *kindness,* BENEFIT, (BENEFACTOR).
Confic-io, ere, *I form, complete, wear out,* (CONFEC-
TIONER). Defic-io, ere, *I fail, revolt,* (DEFICIENT,
DEFECT). Effic-io, ere, *I produce,* EFFECT. Infic-io, ere,
I stain, INFECT. Interfic-io, ere, *I kill.* Malefac-io, ere,
I do ill to. (MALEFACTOR). Offic-io, ere, *I hinder:*
offici-um, i, *duty, service,* OFFICE, (OFFICIOUS). Perfic-io,
ere, *I perform:* perfect-us, a, um, PERFECT. Præfic-io, ere,
I set over, (PREFECT). Profic-io, ere, *I avail,* PROFIT.
Refic-io, ere, *I re-make,* REFIT, *restore.* Satisfac-io, ere,
I SATISFY: Satisfactio, nis, SATISFACTION. Suffic-io,
ere, *I supply,* SUFFICE, (SUFFICIENT).—9. Fall-ax,
acis, *deceitful,* FALLACIOUS. Fals-us, a, um, FALSE.
Refell-o, ere, *I refute.*
421. Famos-us, a, um, *ill-reputed,* FAMOUS. Infam-is, e,
INFAMOUS: infami-a, æ, INFAMY.—3. Famili-a, æ,
slaves of a household, FAMILY: familiar-is, e, *belonging
to the family,* FAMILIAR: familiarit-as, atis, *intimacy,*
FAMILIARITY. — 4. Fanatic-us, a, um, FANATIC.
Profan-us. a, um, PROFANE.—5. Farin-a, æ, *meal, flour.*—
6. Confert-us, a, um, *crowded.* Refert-us, a, um, *filled.*—
7. Nefas, *wrong, impiety:* nefari-us, a, um, *wicked,* NEFA-
B3

8. fasc-is, is, *bundle*.
9. fast-us, us, *pride*.
430. fat-eor, eri, *I own*, (fari).
1. fatig-o, are, *I weary*, FATIGUE, (fătis. obs.)
2. fatu-us, a, um, *silly*, INFATUATED.
3. fav-eo, ēre, I FAVOUR.
4. faust-us, a, um, *propitious*, (faveo).
5. fav-us, i, *honeycomb*.
6. fau-x, cis, *jaw*.
7. fa-x, cis, *torch*.
8. febr-is, is, FEVER.
9. fecund-us, a, um, *fruitful*, (feo, obs.)
440. fel, lis, *gall*.
1. fel-is, is, *cat*.
2. fel-ix, icis, (Adj.) *happy*, (feo).
3. femin-a, æ, *woman*, (feo), (FEMININE).
4. fem-ur, ŏris, *thigh*.
5. fend-o, ĕre, *I strike*, (obs.)
6. fenestr-a, æ, *window*.
7. fen-us, oris, *usury*, (feo.)
8. feri-æ, arum, *holidays*.
9. fer-io, ire, *I strike*.
450. fer-o, re, *I bring*, (irreg.)
1. ferr-um, i, *iron, steel*.

RIOUS.—9. Fastidi-um, i, *disgust, disdain*, (FASTIDIOUS).
430. Confit-eor, eri, I CONFESS. Profit-eor, eri, I PROFESS.
1. Fessus, defessus, a, um, (from fatiscor obs.), *wearied.*—
3. Fav-or, oris, FAVOUR. Fant-or, oris, *favourer.*—
6. Suffoco, are, *I choke*, SUFFOCATE.
442. Felicit-as, atis, *happiness*, FELICITY.— 3. Effeminat-us,
a, um, *womanish*, EFFEMINATE.— 5. Defend-o, ere,
I DEFEND. Offend-o, ere, *I strike on*, OFFEND.—
7. Fener-or, ari, *I lend on usury*.
450. Fer-ax, acis; fertil-is, e, FERTILE. Fer-ox, ocis, *haughty*,
FEROCIOUS. Lat-or, oris, *bringer*, LEGISLATOR.
Affero, *I bring*. Aufero, *I take away*. Confero, *I bring
together, compare*, (CONFER). Defero, *I bring down, offer,
inform*. Differo, *I spread*, DIFFER, DEFER: differenti-a,
æ, DIFFERENCE. Effero, *I bring out, extol, bury*,
(ELATE). Infero, *I bring in, wage*, (INFER). Offero,
I OFFER. Præfero, *I carry before*, PREFER. Profero,
I bring forth, PROFFER. Refero, *I bring back*, REFER,
RELATE: relatio, nis, RELATION, *reference*. Suffero,
I SUFFER. Transfero, I TRANSFER. Translatio, nis,

2. ferv-eo, ēre, *I boil.*
3. fer-us, a, um, *wild,* FIERCE.
4. festin-o, are, *I hasten.*
5. fest-us, a, um, FESTAL.
6. fet-us, us, *produce,* (feo.)
7. fic-us, i, FIG-*tree.*
8. fïd-es, ei, FAITH.
9. fibr-a, æ, FIBRE, *entrail.*
460. fid-es, is, *lute-string.*
1. fig-o, ĕre, I FIX.
2. fili-us, i, *son,* (FILIAL).
3. find-o, ĕre, *I cleave,* (FISSURE).
4. fing-o, ĕre, I FEIGN, *form,* (FICTION).
5. fin-is, is, *end, boundary,* (FINAL).
6. fio, fieri, *I become,* (irreg.)
7. firm-us, a, um, FIRM.
8. flagit-o, are, *I demand.*
9. flagr-o, are, *I burn,* (FLAGRANT).
470. flav-us, a, um, *yellow.*

---

transference, (TRANSLATION).—2. Ferv-or, oris, *heat,* FERVOUR. Fervid-us, a, um, *boiling,* FERVID. Ferment-um, i, *leaven,* FERMENT. Fret-um, i, FRITH.— 5. Fest-um, i, FEAST, FESTIVAL. Festiv-us, a, um, FESTIVE. Infest-us, a, um, *dangerous, hostile :* infest-o, are, *I disquiet,* INFEST.—6. Effet-us, a. um, *past bearing, worn out,* EFFETE.—9. Fïd-us, a, um, fïdel-is, e, *faithful :* fidelit-as, atis, FIDELITY : infidel-is, e, *unfaithful,* INFIDEL. Perfïd-us, a, um, *treacherous,* PERFIDIOUS : perfidi-a, æ, PERFIDY. Fid-o, ere; confid-o, ere, *I trust,* CONFIDE : confidenti-a, æ, CONFIDENCE. Diffid-o, ere, *I distrust :* diffidenti-a, æ, DIFFIDENCE. Fiduci-a, æ, *trust, reliance.*
460. Fidic-en, inis, *lute-player.*--1. Fibul-a, æ, *clasp.* Af, con, de, in, præ, re, suf, trans,-figo.—4. Fictil-is, e, *of earthenware.* Figur-a, æ, FIGURE, *shape.* Figul-us, i, *potter.* Effing-o, ere, *I fashion;* effigi-es, ei, EFFIGY.—5. Fin-io, ire, *I end;* defin-io, ire, *I limit,* DEFINE. Infinit-us, a, um, INFINITE. Affin-is, e, *akin,* (by marriage); affinit-as, atis, AFFINITY. Finitim-us, a, um, *near, adjoininy.* Confin-is, e, *adjoining,* (CONFINE).—7. Firm-o, are, *I establish :* affirm-o, I AFFIRM; confirmo, I CONFIRM. Infirm-us, a, um, INFIRM.—8. Flagiti-um, i, *a scandalous act,* (FLAGITIOUS). —9. Conflagr-o, deflagr-o, *I burn,* (CONFLAGRATION). Flagr-um, i; flagell-um, i, *scourge.* Flamm-a, æ, FLAME : inflamm-o, are, I INFLAME.

1. flect-o, ĕre, *I bend.*
2. fl-eo, ēre, *I weep.*
3. flig-o, ĕre, *I strike,* (obs.)
4. fl-o, are, *I blow.*
5. flo-s, ris, FLOWER.
6. flu-o, ĕre, I FLOW, (FLUENT).
7. foc-us, i, *hearth,* (foveo).
8. fod-io, ĕre, *I dig.*
9. fœd-us, a, um, *foul, ugly.*
480. fœd-us, eris, *treaty,* (CONFEDERATE.)
1. fœn-um, i, *hay.*
2. foli-um, i, *leaf,* (FOLIAGE).
3. fon-s, tis, FOUNTAIN.
4. for, fari, *I speak,* (Def.)
5. for-es, ium, *door.*
6. form-a, æ, *shape,* FORM.
7. formic-a, æ, *ant.*
8. formid-o, ĭnis, *fear.*
9. for-o, are, *I pierce,* (obs.)

471. Floxibil-is, e; flexil-is, e, FLEXIBLE. Inflect-o, ere, *I bend,* (INFLEXION). Reflect-o, ere, *I bend back,* REFLECT, (REFLEXION).— 2. Flet-us, us, *weeping.* Flebil-is, e, *mournful.* Defl-eo, ere, *I bewail.*—3. Afflig-o, ere, *I beat down,* AFFLICT, (AFFLICTION). Config-o, ere, *I engage in battle:* conflict-us, us, CONFLICT. Inflig-o, ere, I INFLICT. Proflig-o, are, *I beat down, worst:* profligat-us, a, um, *ruined,* PROFLIGATE.—4. Flat-us, us, flabr-um, i, flam-en, inis, *blast.* Infl-o, are, I INFLATE. Also, af, con, dif, ef, per, se, suf,-flo.—5. Florid-us, a, um, *blooming,* FLORID. Flor-eo, ēre; floresc-o, ere, *I bloom,* FLOURISH. 6. Fluid-us, a, um, FLUID. Fluvi-us, i; flum-en, inis; fluent-um, i, *river.* Fluct-us, us, *wave, tide:* fluctu-o, are, *I am tossed,* FLUCTUATE. Afflu-o, ere, *I flow to:* affluen-s, tis, AFFLUENT. Conflu-o, ere, *I flow together.* (CONFLUENCE, CONFLUX). Influ-o, ere, *I flow in,* (INFLUENCE). Also, circum, de, dif, ef, præter, pro, re,-fluo.—8. Foss-a, æ, fov-ea, æ, *ditch,* FOSSE. Cou, de, ef, in, per, præ, suf,-fodio.

484. Fat-um, i, FATE: fatal-is, e, FATAL. Affari, *to address:* affabil-is, e, AFFABLE. Infan-s, tis, *speechless,* INFANT. Præfari, *to speak beforehand:* præfatio, nis, PREFACE. Also, ef, pro,-fari.— 5. Foris, *abroad,* (FOREIGN). Foras, *out of doors.*—6. Form-o, are, *I form.* Deform-is, e, *ugly,* DEFORMED. Con, de, in, trans,-formo, (INFORM, TRANSFORM, &c.).—8. Formid-o. are, *I fear,* (FORMIDABLE).—9. Perfor-o, are, *I bore through,* PERFORATE. Foram-en, inis, *hole, crevice.*

490. for-s, tis, *chance*, (fero).
  1. fort-is, e, *brave*, (fero).
  2. for-um, i, *market, court.*
  3. fov-eo, ēre, *I cherish.*
  4. fragr-o, are, *I smell sweet*, (FRAGRANT).
  5. frang-o, ĕre, *I break*, (FRACTURE).
  6. frat-er, ris, BROTHER.
  7. frau-s, dis, *deceit*, FRAUD.
  8. fraxin-us, i, *ash-tree.*
  9. frem-o, ĕre, *I bellow.*
500. fren-um, i, *bit.*
  1. frequen-s, tis, (Adj.) FREQUENT, *full.*
  2. fret-us, a, um, *relying.*
  3. fric-o, are, *I rub*, (FRICTION).
  4. frig-us, ŏris, *cold.*
  5. frivol-us, a, um, *slight*, FRIVOLOUS.
  6. fron-s, tis, *brow*, FRONT.
  7. fron-s, dis, *leaf.*
  8. fru-or, i, *I enjoy.*
  9. frustra, *vainly.*
510. frut-ex, ĭcis, *shrub.*
  1. fug-io, ĕre, *I flee.*
  2. fulc-io, ire, *I prop.*

490. Forsan, forsitan, fortasse, *perhaps.* Forte, *by chance :* fortuit-us, a, um, *casual.* Fortun-a, æ, FORTUNE.—1. Fortitud-o, inis, *bravery*, FORTITUDE.—3. Foment-um, i, *poultice*, FOMENTATION.—5. Fragil-is, e, FRAGILE, FRAIL. Fragment-um, i, FRAGMENT. Frag-or, oris, *roar.* Infring-o, ere, *I break in*, INFRINGE. Suffragi-um, i, *vote*, SUFFRAGE. Suffrag-or, ari, *I vote for.* Refrag-or, ari, *I vote against.* Also, con, ef, de, per, præ, re. suf, -fringo.—6. Fratern-us, a, um, *brotherly*, FRATERNAL.—7. Fraudulent-us, a, um, FRAUDULENT. Fraud-o, defraud-o, are, I DEFRAUD.—8. Fremit-us, us, *bellowing.*

500. Fren-o, are; refren-o, are, *I curb.* Effren-us; effrenat-us, a, um, *unbridled.* Frequenti-a, æ, FREQUENCY, *full attendance.* Frequent-o, are, I FREQUENT.—4. Frigid-us, a, um, *cold :* frig-eo, ere; frigesc-o, ere, *I grow cold, am cold,* FREEZE.—5. Frond-eo, ere; frondesc-o, ere, *I am in leaf.*—6. Fruct-us, us, FRUIT. Frument-um, i, *corn.* Fru-x, gis, *fruit.* Frugal-is, e, FRUGAL.—9. Frustr-or, ari, I FRUSTRATE.

511. Fug-a, æ, *flight.* Fugitiv-us, a, um, FUGITIVE. An, con, de, dif, ef, per, pro, re, subter, suf, trans,-fugio. Refugi-um, i, REFUGE. (SUBTERFUGE).—2. Fulcr-um, i, *prop.*—

3. fulg-eo, ēre, *I shine.*
4. fulv-us, a, um, *tawny.*
5. fum-us, i, *smoke.*
6. fund-a, æ, *sling.*
7. fund-o, ēre, *I pour.*
8. fund-us, i, *bottom, farm.*
9. fung-or, i, *I perform.*
520. fun-is, is, *rope.*
1. fun-us, ĕris, FUNERAL.
2. fur, is, *thief.*
3. furc-a, æ, FORK, (fero.)
4. furn-us, i, *oven,* FURNACE.
5. fur-o, ĕre, *I rage.*
6. fusc-us, a, um, *dun.*
7. fust-is, is, *club.*
8. futil-is, e, FUTILE.
9. fut-o, are, *I argue,* (obs.)
530. Gale-a, æ, *helmet.*
1. gall-us, i, *cock.*
2. garr-io, ire, *I chatter.*
3. gaud-eo, ēre, *I rejoice.*
4. gel-u, u, *frost.*
5. gemin-us, a, um, *double, twin.*
6. gemma, æ, *jewel,* GEM.
7. gem-o, ēre, *I groan.*

3. Fulg-or, oris, *glitter.* Fulgur, is, *lightning.* Fulm-en, inis, *thunderbolt.* Ef, præ, re,-fulgeo. (EFFULGENT, REFULGENT).—5. Fum-o, are, *I smoke.*—7. Af, con, de, dif, ef, in, of, per, pro, re, suf, trans,-fundo, (CONFOUND, CONFUSE, DIFFUSION, INFUSE, &c.)—8. Funditus, *utterly.* Fund-o, are, I FOUND : fundament-um, i, FOUNDATION, (FUNDAMENTAL). Profund-us, a, um, *deep,* PROFOUND. —9. Functio, nis, FUNCTION. Defung-or, i, *I discharge,* (DEFUNCT). Perfung-or, i, *I perform.*

520. Funal-e, is, *string, rope.*—1. Funere-us, a, um ; funebr-is, e, FUNEREAL. Funest-us, a, um, *mournful,, fatal.*—2. Fur-or, ari, *I steal.* Furt-um, i, *theft.* Furtiv-us, a, um, *stealthy.* FURTIVE.—5. Fur-or, oris, *rage, madness.* Furi-a, æ, FURY. Furios-us, a, um, FURIOUS.—9. Confut-o, are, I CONFUTE. Refut-o, are, I REFUTE.

531. Gallin-a, æ, *hen.*—2. Garrul-us, a, um, *prating,* GARRULOUS.—3. Gaudi-um, i, *joy.*—4. Gelid-us, a, um, *frozen.* Glaci-es, ei, *ice.* Congel-o, are, I CONGEAL.—5. Gemin-o, are, *I double.*—7. Gemit-us, us, *groan, lamentation.* Con, in,

8. gen-a, æ, *cheek.*
9. gen-s, tis, *nation, clan*, (gigno).
540. gen-u, u, KNEE.
1. germ-en, inis, *sprout*, (gigno).
2. ger-o, ĕre, *I bear, perform, behave.*
3. gign-o, ĕre, I ENGENDER.
4. gladi-us, i, *sword.*
5. glan-s, dis, *acorn.*
6. gleb-a, æ, *soil,* GLEBE.
7. glob-us, i, GLOBE.
8. glori-a, æ, GLORY.
9. gnar-us, a, um, *knowing.*
550. gnav-us, a, um, *active.*
1. gracil-is, e, *slender.*
2. grad-us, us, *step,* GRADE.

-gemo. — 9. Gentil-is, e, *belonging to a clan,* (GENTILE, GENTLE, GENTLEMAN).
541. German-us, a, *related in blood, brother (sister), cousin,* -GERMAN.—2. Gest-us, us, *bearing,* GESTURE. Gest-io, ire, *I delight, desire.* Diger-o, ere, I DIGEST. Sugger-o, ere, *I supply,* SUGGEST. Also, con, e, in,-gero.—3. Genuin-us, a, um, GENUINE. Gen-us, eris, *kind, race, family:* general-is, e, GENERAL. Generos-us, a, um, *nobly born,* GENEROUS: gener-o, are, I ENGENDER, (GENERATION): degener, is, DEGENERATE. Genit-or, oris, *father.* Geni-us, i, *guardian-spirit, natural inclination:* genial-is, e, GENIAL, (CONGENIAL). Gener, i, *son-in-law.* Ingign-o, ere, *I engender in:* ingenu-us, a, um, *free-born, noble,* INGENUOUS: ingeni-um, i, *talent, character,* GENIUS: ingenios-us, a, um, *talented,* INGENIOUS, (INGENUITY): indigen-a, æ, *native,* INDIGENOUS. Progign-o, ere, *I beget;* progeni-es, ei, *offspring,* PROGENY: progenit-or, oris, PROGENITOR. — 4. Gladiat-or, oris, *swordsman.*—5. Juglan-s, dis, *walnut.*—8. Glorios-us, a, um, GLORIOUS, VAINGLORIOUS. Glori-or, ari, *I boast, glory.*—9. Ignar-us, a, um, *unknowing.* Iguor-o, are, *I am* IGNORANT: ignoranti-a, æ, IGNORANCE.
550. Ignav-us, a, um, *lazy, cowardly;* ignavi-a, æ, *laziness, cowardice.* Nav-o, are, *I perform.*—2. Grad-ior, i, *I step, go;* gress-us, us, *step:* grass-or, ari, *I go eagerly;* aggred-ior, i, *I approach, attempt, attack,* (AGGRESSION): congred-ior, i, *I meet, engage:* congress-us, us, *meeting,* CONGRESS: digred-ior, i, *I go apart,* DIGRESS: egred-ior, i, *I go out:* egress-us, us, EGRESS: ingred-ior, *I enter, begin:* ingress-us, us, *entrance,* INGRESS: progred-ior, i, *I go forward;* progress-us, us, PROGRESS: trangred-ior, *I cross,* TRANS-

3. gram-en, inis, *grass.*
4. grand-is, e, *great,* GRAND.
5. grand-o, ĭnis, *hail.*
6. gran-um, i, GRAIN.
7. grat-us, a, um, *pleasing,* GRATEFUL.
8. grav-is, e, *heavy, important,* GRAVE.
9. gremi-um, i, *lap.*
560. gre-x, gis, *flock.*
1. gubern-o, are, I GOVERN.
2. gust-o, are, *I taste.*
3. gutt-a, æ, *drop.*
4. guttur, is, *throat.*
5. Hab-eo, ēre, I HAVE.
6. habit-o, are, *I dwell,* INHABIT, (habeo).
7. hær-eo, ēre, *I stick.*
8. hal-o, are, *I breathe.*
9. ham-us, i, *hook.*
570. harusp-ex, ĭcis, *soothsàyer.*
1. hast-a, æ, *spear.*
2. haud, *not.*
3. haur-io, ire, *I draw, drain.*
4. heb-es, ĕtis, (Adj.) *dull.*
5. heder-a, æ, *ivy.*
6. hei, heu, *alas.*

GRESS. Also, intro, præ, re,-gredior.—7. Grati-a, æ, *favour,* GRACE, *thanks.* Grat-or, gratul-or, congratul-or, ari, *I wish joy,* CONGRATULATE. Gratific-or, ari, *I present,* GRATIFY. Ingrat-us, a, um, *unpleasant, ungrateful.*—8. Gravit-as, atis, *weightiness, seriousness,* GRAVITY. Gravid-us, a, um, *big, pregnant.* Grav-o, are, *I weigh down :* grav-or, ari, *I grudge.* Ag, de, in, præ,-gravo, (AGGRAVATE). Ingravesc-o, ere, *I grow weary, or serious.*
560. Congreg-o, are, *I collect,* CONGREGATE. Egregi-us, a, um, *distinguished, eminent,* EGREGIOUS. Also, ag, se,-grego.—1. Gubernacul-um, i, *rudder.* — 2. Gust-us, us, *taste.*—5. Haben-a, æ, *rein.* Habil-is, e, *skilful.* Habit-us, us, *fashion,* HABIT : habitud-o, inis, HABITUDE. Adhib-eo, ere, *I apply.* Cohib-eo, *I restrain.* Exhib-eo, *I deliver,* EXHIBIT. Præb-eo, *I afford.* Probib-eo, *I prevent,* PROHIBIT. Also, in, per, red,-hibeo.—7. Hæsit-o, are, *I stick,* HESITATE. Ad, co, in,-bæreo,-hæresco, (ADHERE, COHESION, INHERENT, &c.).—8. Halit-us, us, *breath.* Anhel-o, are, *I pant.* Exhal-o, *I breathe out,* EXHALE.
573. Haust-us, us, *draught.* Exhaur-io, ire, *I draw forth,*

7. herb-a, æ, HERB, *grass.*
8. her-es, edis, HEIR.
9. heri, *yesterday.*
580. hero-s, is, HERO.
  1. her-us, i, *master.*
  2. hic, hæc, hoc, *this.*
  3. hiem-s, is, *winter.*
  4. hilar-is, e, *merry.*
  5. hi-o, are, *I gape.*
  6. hirsut-us, a, um, *shaggy.*
  7. hirund-o, ĭnis, *swallow.*
  8. hœd-us, i, *kid.*
  9. hom-o, ĭnis, *man.*
590. hon-or, ōris, HONOUR.
  1. hor-a, æ, HOUR.
  2. horr-eo, ēre, *I shudder.*
  3. hort-or, ari, *I exhort.*
  4. hort-us, i, *garden,* (HORTICULTURE).
  5. hosp-es, ĭtis, HOST, *guest.*
  6. host-is, is, *enemy.*
  7. hum-eo, ēre, *I am moist.*
  8. humer-us, i, *shoulder.*
  9. hum-us, i, *ground.*
600. Jac-eo, ēre, *I lie down.*
  1. jac-io, ĕre, *I cast.*

EXHAUST. — 8. Heredit-as, atis, INHERITANCE, HERITAGE, (HEREDITARY).—9. Hestern-us, a, um, YESTER.
582. Hic, *here.* Huc, *hither:* adhuc, *yet, hitherto.* Hinc, *hence.* Hactenus, *thus far.*—3. Hibern-us, a, um, *wintry.*—5. Hiāt-us, us, *yawn, gap.*—9. Human-us, a, um, HUMAN, HUMANE, *polite:* humanit-as, atis, *politeness,* HUMANITY.
590. Honor-o, are, *I honour.* Honest-us, a, um, HONORABLE, *virtuous,* (HONEST).—2. Horrid-us, a, um, *rough, bristling,* HORRID. Horribĭl-is, e, HORRIBLE. Horr-or, oris, *shuddering,* HORROUR. Abhorr-eo, ere, I ABHOR.— 3. Ad, co, ex,-hortor, I EXHORT.—4. Hort-i, orum, *pleasure-garden.*— 5. Hospital-is, e, HOSPITABLE. Hospitalit-as, atis, HOSPITALITY. Hospiti-um, i, *hospitality, reception, inn.*—6. Hostil-is, e, HOSTILE.—7. Humid-us, a, um, *moist.* Hum-or, oris, *moisture.*—9. Humil-is, e, *lowly,* HUMBLE: humilit-as, atis, *lowness,* HUMILITY. Hum-o, are, *I inter.*
600. Adjac-eo, ere, *I lie near,* (ADJACENT). Also, circum, inter, ob, sub,-jaceo.—1. Jacul-um, i, JAVELIN: jacul-or,

C

2. jam, *now, already.*
3. janu-a, æ, *gate,* (Janus).
4. ibi, *there.*
5. ict-us, us, *stroke,* (ico).
6. idone-us, a, um, *fit.*
7. idu-o, *I divide,* (obs).
8. igitur, *therefore.*
9. ign-is, is, *fire.*
610. ill-e, a, ud, *that, he.*
1. imag-o, ïnis, IMAGE (IMAGINE, IMAGINA-
2. imb-er, ris, *shower.* [TION).
3. imit-or, ari, I IMITATE.
4. imman-is, e, *huge.*
5. in, IN, *into.*
6. inan-is, e, *empty.*
7. indulg-eo, ēre, I INDULGE.
8. industri-us, a, um, INDUSTRIOUS.
9. infer-us, a, um, *low, placed beneath.*
620. ingeni-um, i, *ability, disposition,* (ingigno).
1. ingen-s, tis, (Adj.) *vast; mighty.*
2. inquam,, *say I,* (Def.)
3. instar, *import, likeness,* (Def.)
4. insul-a, æ, ISLAND.
5. integ-er, ra, rum, ENTIRE, *pure.*

ari, *I dart :* ejacul-or, *I dart forth,* (EJACULATE). Jact-us,
us, *cast.* Jactur-a, æ, *loss.* Jact-o, are, *I cast.* Abjic-io,
I cast away : abject-us, a, um, *cast off,* ABJECT. Adjic-io,
I add. Conjic-io, *I throw, drive, guess :* conjectur-a, æ, *guess,*
CONJECTURE. Dejic-io, *I cast down ;* deject-us, a, um,
cast down, DEJECTED. Ejic-io, *I cast out,* EJECT. Injic-io,
I cast in, INJECT. Objic-io, *I cast against,* OBJECT :
obj-ex or ob-ex, icis, *bolt, bar.* Projic-io, *I cast forward,* or
forth, PROJECT. Rejic-io, *I cast back,* REJECT. Subjic-io,
I cast under, (SUBJECT). Transjic-io, *I cast over.*—
3. Janit-or, oris, *gate-keeper, porter.*—7. Id-us, uum, IDES,
(of a Roman month). Vidu-us, a, um, WIDOWED. Divid-o,
ere, I DIVIDE.
610. Illic, *there.* Illuc, *thither.* Illino, *thence.* — 5. Inde,
thence.—7. Indulgenti-a, æ, INDULGENCE.—8. Industri-a,
æ, INDUSTRY.—9. Infer-i, orum, *shades, gods of hell ;*
inferi-æ, arum, *offerings to shades or gods below.* Inferi-or,
us, *lower,* INFERIOR : infim-us, or im-us, a, um, *lowest :*
immo, *yes, nay but, nay more.* Infra, *below.* Infern-us, a, um,
INFERNAL.
620. Ingenios-us, a, um, *talented,* INGENIOUS.—3. Instaur-o
and restaur-o, are, *I renew,* RESTORE.—5. Integrit-as, atis,

6. inter, *between, among.*
7. interpr-es, ĕtis, INTERPRETER.
8. intus, *within.*
9. invit-o, are, I INVITE.
630. invit-us, a, um, *unwilling.*
1. joc-us, i, JOKE, *jest.*
2. ir-a, æ, *anger,* IRE.
3. irrit-o, are, *I provoke,* IRRITATE, (ira).
4. is, ea, id, *that.*
5. ita, *so.*
6. iterum, *again.*
7. jub-eo, ēre, *I command.*
8. jucund-us, a, um, *pleasant,* JOCUND, (juvo).
9. jud-ex, icis, JUDGE, (jus dico).
640. jung-o, ĕre, I JOIN.
1. jur-o, are, *I swear,* (jus).
2. jus, juris, *right, law.*

entireness, INTEGRITY. Integr-o and redintegr-o, are, *I renew, refresh.*—6. Interim, *meanwhile.* Interdum, *between whiles, sometimes.*—7. Interpret-or, ari, I INTERPRET.—8. Interi-or, us, *inner,* INTERIOR: intim-us, a, um, *inmost.* Intro, *within.* Intra, *within.* Intestin-us, a, um, INTESTINE. Intr-o, are, I ENTER.—9. Invitatio, nis, INVITATION.

631. Jocos-us, a, um, *funny,* JOCOSE. Joc-or, ari, *I joke, jest.*—2. Irasc-or, i, *I am angry:* iracund-us, a, um, *passionate, angry.*—4. Eò, *thither:* ideo, *therefore:* ist-e, a, ud, *that one.* Idem, eadem, ìdem, *the same,* IDENTICAL. Ips-e, a, um, *self, very.*—4. Itaque, *and so, therefore.*—6. Iter-o, are, *I repeat,* REITERATE.—7. Juss-um, i, *command.*—9. Jud-ico, are, I JUDGE: judici-um, i, *judgment, trial, court of justice:* adjudic-o, are, I ADJUDGE: dijudic-o, are, *I decide:* præjudic-o, are, I PREJUDGE: præjudici-um, i, PRE-JUDGMENT, PREJUDICE.

640. Junctur-a, æ, *joining,* JUNCTURE. Jug-um, i, *yoke:* jug-o, are, *I yoke:* conjug-o, *I yoke together,* CONJUGATE: big-æ, æ, (for bijuga) *chariot and pair:* quadrig-a, æ, (for quadrijuga) *chariot and four.* Jug-is, e, *running* (water). Jugul-um, i, *throat;* jugul-o, are, *I cut a throat, murder,* (JUGULAR vein). Jument-um, i, *beast of burthen.* Juxta, *adjoining, near.* Ad, con, dis, in, sub,-jungo, I AD—CON—DIS—EN—SUB—JOIN: conj-ux, ugis, *a wedded person, husband or wife:* conjugi-um, i, *wedlock,* (CONJUGAL).—1. Abjur-o, I ABJURE. Adjur-o, I ADJURE. Conjur-o, *I conspire:* conjuratio, nis, *conspiracy.* Perjuro, or pejero, *I forswear:* perjuri-um, i, PERJURY. — 2. Just-us, a, um, JUST: justiti-a, æ, JUSTICE: justiti-um, i, *cessation of law-courts,*

3. jus, juris, *sauce, gravy.*
4. juven-is, is, *a young person, young.*
5. juv-o, are, *I help, I delight.*
6. Lăb-or, i, *I slide, glide, fall.*
7. lăb-or, oris, *toil,* LABOUR.
8. labr-um, i, *lip,* (lambo).
9. lac, tis, *milk.*
650. lacer, a, um, *torn.*
1. lacert-us, i, *arm.*
2. lac-io, ere, *I entice,* (obs.)
3. lacrym-a, æ, *tear.*
4. lac-us, us, LAKE.
5. læd-o, ĕre, *I hurt.*
6. læt-us, a, um, *joyful.*
7. læv-us, a, um, LEFT, *unpropitious.*
8. lamb-o, ere, *I lick.*
9. lament-or, ari, I LAMENT.
660. lan-a, æ, *wool.*
1. langu-eo, ēre, I LANGUISH.
2. lan-x, cis, *dish, scale.*
3. lap-is, ĭdis, *stone.*
4. laque-us, i, *snare.*

vacation. Jurisdictio, nis, JURISDICTION. (JURIS-
PRUDENCE). Injuri-a, æ, *wrong,* INJURY : injurios-us, a,
um, INJURIOUS. Jurg-or, ari, *I quarrel, wrangle ;* objurg-o,
are, *I reproach.*—4. Juvenil-is, e, *youthful,* JUVENILE.
Juvent-us, utis, and -a, æ, *youth.* Juvenc-us, i, *bullock.*—
5. Adjuv-o, are, *I help :* adjut-or, oris, *helper,* COADJUTOR :
adjument-um, i, *assistance.*—6. Laps-us, us, *fall,* LAPSE.
Lab-es, is, *fall, ruin, stain.* Lab-o, are, *I totter :* labefac-io,
ere, *I shake, undermine.* Al, col, de, di, e, il, per, præter, pro,
sub, subter,-labor.—7. Laborios-us, a, um, LABORIOUS.
Labor-o, are, *I labour.*
650. Lacer-o, dilacer-o, are, *I tear,* LACERATE.—2. Lacess-o,
ere, *I provoke.* Lact-o, are, *I tice.* Allic-io, ere, *I allure.*
Delici-æ, arum, DELIGHTS, DELICACIES: delicat-us, a,
um, DELICATE: delect-o, are, I DELIGHT. Elic-io, ere,
I tice out, ELICIT. Illic-io, ere, *I entice :* illecebr-a, æ,
allurement. Oblect-o, are, *I amuse, delight.* Pellic-io, ere,
I allure. Lacun-ar or laque-ar, aris, *ceiling.*—5. Al, il,-lid-o,
ere, *I dash upon.* Collid-o, ere, *I dash together,* (COLLISION).
Elid-o, ere, *I crush out, weaken.*—6. Læt-or, ari, *I rejoice.*
Lætiti-a, æ, *joy.* — 9. Lament-um, i ; lamentatio, nis,
LAMENTATION.
660. Lanug-o, inis, *down.*—1. Languid-us, a, um, LANGUID.
Langu-or, oris, LANGUOUR.—4. Illaque-o, are, *I ensnare.*—

5. larg-us, a, um, *bounteous, abundant,* LARGE.
6. lass-us, a, um, *weary.*
7. lat-eo, ēre, *I lie hid,* (LATENT).
8. latr-o, are, *I bark.*
9. latro, nis, *robber.*
670. lat-us, a, um, *wide, broad.*
  1. lat-us, ĕris, *side.*
  2. laur-us, i, *bay-tree,* LAUREL.
  3. lau-s, dis, *praise.*
  4. lav-o, are, *I wash,* LAVE.
  5. lax-us, a, um, *loose,* LAX.
  6. lect-us, i, *couch.*
  7. lēg-o, are, *I dispatch, send.*
  8. lĕg-o, ĕre, *I gather, read.*
  9. len-is, e, *gentle.*
680. lent-us, a, um, *pliant, slow.*
  1. l-eo, ēre, *I smear.* (obs.)
  2. leo, nis, LION.
  3. lep-or, ōris, *wit, elegance.*

5. Larg-ior, iri, *I bestow, give* LARGESS.—6. Lassitud-o, inis, *weariness,* LASSITUDE. Lass-o, are, *I weary.*—7. Latebr-a, æ, *hiding-place.*—9. Latrocin-or, ari, *I rob:* latrocini-um, i, *robbery.*
670. Latè, *widely.* Latitud-o, inis, *width,* LATITUDE. Dilat-o, are, *I extend,* DILATE.—3. Laud-o, are, *I praise,* LAUD. Laudabil-is, e, *praiseworthy,* LAUDABLE.—4. Laut-us, a, um, *sumptuous.*—5. Lax-o, relax-o, are, *I loosen,* RELAX. Lasciv-us, a, um, *wanton.* Prolix-us, a, um, *long,* PROLIX, *easy.*—6. Lectic-a, æ, *litter, sedan.*—7. Legat-us, i, *ambassador, lieutenant,* LEGATE. Colleg-a, æ, COLLEAGUE: collegi-um, i, COLLEGE. Legat-um, i, LEGACY. Ableg-o, are, *I dismiss.* Deleg-o, are, I DELEGATE. Releg-o, are, *I banish.* — 8. Legio, nis, LEGION. Lectio, nis, *choice, reading.* Lect-or, oris, *reader.* Collig-o, ere, I COLLECT. Delig-o, ere, *I choose;* delect-us, us, *choice, levy.* Dilig-o, ere, *I distinguish, love:* diligen-s, tis, *careful,* DILIGENT: diligenti-a, æ, DILIGENCE. Elig-o, ere, *I choose,* ELECT: elegan-s, tis, ELEGANT. Intellig-o, ere, *I understand:* intelligen-s, tis, INTELLIGENT. Neglig-o, ere, I NEGLECT: negligen-s, tis, NEGLIGENT. Perleg-o, ere, *I read through.* Releg-o, ere, *I re-read, I recover.* Selig-o, ere, I SELECT. — 9. Lenit-as, atis, *gentleness,* LENITY. Len-io, ire, *I soften,* (LENIENT); lenim-en, inis; leniment-um, i, *assuagement.*
681. Del-eo, ere, *I blot out.* Lin-o, ere, *I smear:* litur-a, æ, *blot, erasure.* Al, circum, il, ob, sub,-lino.—3. Lepid-us, a, um,

c3

4. lep-us, ŏris, *hare.*
5. let-um, i, *death,* (Lethe).
6. lĕv-is, e, *light, slight, fickle.*
7. lēv-is, e, *smooth.*
8. lex, legis, LAW,(lĕgo),(LEGAL,LEGISLATOR).
9. līber, a, um, *free.*
690. lĭb-er, ri, *bark, book,* (LIBRARY).
  1. Līber, i, *Bacchus.*
  2. lib-et, or lub-et, ēre, *it pleaseth,* (Impers.)
  3. lib-o, are, *I pour, sip.*
  4. libr-a, æ, *balance.*
  5. lic-et, ēre, *it is allowed,* (Impers.)
  6. lign-um, i, *wood.*
  7. lig-o, are, *I bind,* (LICTOR).
  8. ligo, nis, *spade.*
  9. lili-um, i, LILY.
700. lim-a, æ, *file.*
  1. lim-en, ĭnis, *threshold.*
  2. lim-es, ĭtis, *boundary,* LIMIT.
  3. limpid-us, a, um, *clear,* LIMPID, (lympha).
  4. lim-us, i, *mud,* SLIME.
  5. line-a, æ, LINE, (linum).
  6. lingu-a, æ, *tongue,* LANGUAGE.

witty, elegant.— 5. Letal-is, e, *deadly.*— 6. Levit-as, atis, *lightness,* LEVITY, *fickleness.* Lev-o, allev-o, relev-o, are, *I lighten,* RELIEVE, ALLEVIATE. Levam-en, inis, levament-um, i, RELIEF. Elev-o, are, *I raise,* ELEVATE, *depreciate.* Sublev-o, are, *I assist, relieve.*—8. Legitim-us, a, um, *lawful,* LEGITIMATE.— 9. Liber-i, orum, *free-born children.* Libert-as, atis, *freedom,* LIBERTY. Liberal-is, e, *belonging to freemen,* LIBERAL : liberalit-as, atis, LIBERALITY. Liber-o, are, *I set free,* LIBERATE. Libert-us, i, *freedman :* libertin-us, a, um, *belonging to freedmen,* of *freedman class.* Deliber-o, are, I DELIBERATE.
690. Libell-us, *small book,* (LIBEL).— 2. Libit-us, us, *choice.* Libid-o, inis, *desire, lust.* — 3. Libatio, nis, libam-en, inis, libament-um, i, *libation.* Delib-o, are, *I sip.*—4. Libr-o, are, *I poise.*—5. Licenti-a, æ, LICENCE, LICENTIOUSNESS. Lic-eo, ere, *I am bid for.* Lic-eor, eri, and licit-or, ari, *I bid for :* licitatio, nis, *bidding.* Pollic-eor, eri, *I promise.*— 7. Oblig-o, are, *I bind down,* OBLIGE : obligatio, nis, OBLIGATION. Al, col, de, il, præ, re, sub,-lig-o, are.
700. Lim-o, are, *I polish.*—5. Line-o, deline-o, are, *I sketch,* DELINEATE. Lineament-um, i, LINEAMENT.—6. Ling-o,

7. linqu-o, ĕre, *I leave.*
8. lin-um, i, *flax*, (LINEN).
9. liqu-eo, ĕre, *I am flowing, I melt.*
710. lis, litis, *strife.*
  1. liter-a, æ, LETTER, (lino), (OBLITERATE).
  2. lit-us, ŏris, *shore.*
  3. loc-us, i, *place*, (LOCAL).
  4. long-us, a, um, LONG.
  5. loqu-or, i, *I speak.*
  6. lor-um, i, *thong.*
  7. lubric-us, a, um, *slippery.*
  8. lucr-um, i, *gain*, LUCRE, (LUCRATIVE).
  9. luct-or, ari, *I struggle, wrestle.*
720. luc-us, i, *grove.*
  1. lud-us, i, *play, game.*
  2. lug-eo, ēre, *I mourn.*
  3. lum-en, ĭnis, *light*, (luceo), (LUMINOUS, LUMINARY).
  4. lun-a, æ, *moon*, (luceo), (LUNAR).
  5. lu-o, ere, *I loose, cleanse, atone.*

ere; ligur-io, ire, I LICK.—7. Delinqu-o, ere, *I err;* delict-um, i, *fault, transgression*, (DELINQUENT). Relinqu-o, ere, *I leave*, RELINQUISH, (RELICT): reliqu-us, a, um, *remaining:* relliqui-æ, arum, *remnant*, RELICS: derelinqu-o, ere, *I desert:* derelictio, nis, *desertion*, DERELICTION.— 8. Linte-um, i, *towel.*—9. Liquesc-o, ere, *I melt.* Liquet, *it is clear.* Liquid-us, a, um, LIQUID. Liqu-or, oris, LIQUOR, *clearness.*

710. Litig-o, are, *I go to law*, LITIGATE: litigios-us, a, um, LITIGIOUS.—1. Liter-æ, arum, *letters*, LITERATURE: literat-us, a, um, LETTERED, LITERARY.—3. Locul-us, i, *chest, casket.* Loc-o, colloc-o, are, *I place.* Locupl-es, etis, *wealthy.* Eloc-o, *I let out.* Illico, *on the spot, forthwith.*— 4. Longè, *afar.* Longitud-o, inis, *length*, (LONGITUDE). Longinqu-us, a, um, *far distant.*—5. Loqu-ax, acis, *talkative*, LOQUACIOUS. Locutio, nis, *saying.* Al, col, e, pro,-loquor. Colloqui-um, i, *conversation*, COLLOQUY. Eloquen-s, tis, ELOQUENT: eloquenti-a, æ, ELOQUENCE; elocutio, nis, ELOCUTION. Obloqu-or, i, *I speak against*, (OBLOQUY). —6. Loric-a, æ, *leathern breastplate.*

721. Lud-o, ere, *I play:* lus-us, us, *sport, play.* Allud-o, *I play on*, (ALLUDE, ALLUSION). Collud-o, *I play with*, (COLLUDE, COLLUSION); elud-o, I ELUDE; illudo, *I mock, play upon*, (ILLUSION). Prolud-o, ere, *I play beforehand.* Ludibri-um, i, *mockery.* Ludicr-us, a, um, LUDICROUS.— 2. Lugubr-is, e, *mournful.* Luct-us, us, *mourning:* luctuos-us, a, um, *mournful.*—5. Lu-es, is, *blight, taint.* Lut-um, i, *mud.*

32

6. lup-us, i, *wolf*.
7. lurid-us, a, um, LURID, *pale*.
8. lusc-us, a, um, *one-eyed*.
9. lu-x, cis, LIGHT.
730. lux-us, us, *luxury*.
1. lymph-a, æ, *water*.
2. lyr-a, æ, LYRE.
3. Mac-er, ra, rum, *lean*.
4. machin-a, æ, MACHINE.
5. macul-a, æ, *stain, spot*.
6. mad-eo, ēre, *I am wet*.
7. magist-er, ri, MASTER, (magnus).
8. magn-us, a, um, *great*.
9. mag-us, i, MAGICIAN.
740. malle-us, i, *hammer*, MALLET.
1. mal-us, i, *apple-tree*.
2. mal-us, i, *mast*.
3. mal-us, a, um, *bad*.

Lustr-um, i, *lair*. Lustr-um, i, *sin-offering, atonement, period of 5 years:* lustr-o, are, *I purify, survey, traverse:* col, per, -lustro: lustratio, nis, *purifying*, LUSTRATION. Abluo, *I cleanse by washing*, (ABLUTION). Alluo, *I wash by*, (ALLUVIAL). Colluo, *I cleanse:* colluvi-es, ei, *commixture*. Diluo, *I wash out*, (DILUTE): diluvi-es, ei, DELUGE. Polluo, I POLLUTE. E, per, pro, sub,-luo.—6. Lupin-us, i, and um, i, *wolf-bean*, LUPIN.—9. Lucid-us, a, um, *bright*, LUCID. Luc-eo, ere, *I shine:* col, di, e, per,-luceo: diluculum, i, *morning-dawn:* pellucid-us, a, um, *transparent, pellucid*. Lucern-a, æ, *lamp*. Lucubr-o, are, *I work at night:* (LUCUBRATION). Luculent-us, a, um, *bright, good, respectable*. Lucifer, a, um, *light-bringing*, (*morning-star*). Lustr-o, are, *I enlighten*, (LUSTRE): col, il,-lustro, *I enlighten. light up*, ILLUSTRATE: illustr-is, e, ILLUSTRIOUS.
730. Luxuri-a, æ, LUXURY: luxurios-us, a, um, LUXURIOUS: luxuri-o, are, *I wanton*, LUXURIATE.—2. Lyric-us, a, um, LYRIC.—3. Maci-es, ei, *leanness, consumption*, (EMACIATED). —4. Machin-or, ari, *I contrive, plot*, (MACHINATION).— 5. Maculos-us, a, um, *full of stains*. Macul-o, are, *I stain.*— 6. Madid-us, a, um, *wet*.—7. Magistr-a, æ, MISTRESS. Magistrat-us, us, *public office*, (MAGISTRATE). 8. Magnitud-o, inis, *size*, MAGNITUDE. Magnanim-us, a, um, MAGNANIMOUS: magnanimit-as, atis, MAGNANIMITY. magnific-us, a, um, MAGNIFICENT: magnificenti-a, æ, MAGNIFICENCE. Magnopere, *greatly*. Majest-as, atis, MAJESTY, (MAJESTIC). Mag-is, *more*.—9. Magic-us, a, um, MAGIC.
741. Măl-um, i, *apple*.—3. Măl-um, i, *evil*, (MALADY). Male,

4. mamm-a, æ, *breast.*
5. mand-o, ate, I COMMAND, *commit*, (DEMAND).
6. mane, *in the morning*, (Def.)
7. man-eo, ere, *I await*, REMAIN.
8. manifest-us, a, um, *evident*, MANIFEST, (manus).
9. man-o, are, *I trickle.*
750. man-us, us, *hand, troop.*
1. marc-eo, ēre, *I wither.*
2. mar-e, is, *sea.*
3. marg-o, ïnis, MARGIN.
4. marmor, is, MARBLE, *sea.*
5. mas, maris, MALE.
6. mat-er, ris, MOTHER.
7. materi-a, æ, MATTER, (MATERIAL).
8. matur-us, a, um, *ripe, early*, MATURE.
9. med-eor, eri, *I heal.*
760. medit-or, ari, *I consider, practice*, MEDITATE.
1. medi-us, a, um, MIDDLE, (MEDIATE, MEDIATOR).
2. medull-a, æ, *marrow.*

badly, ill. Malign-us, a, um, MALIGNANT: malignit-as, atis, MALIGNITY. Maliti-a, æ, *wickedness*, MALICE: malitios-us, a, um, MALICIOUS.—5. Mandat-um, i, MANDATE, *message.* Commend-o, are, *I entrust*, COMMEND, RECOMMEND.—6. Matutin-us, a, um, *happening in the morning.*—7. Mansio, nis, *residence*, MANSION. Per, re, -maneo.—9. Eman-o, are, *I ooze forth*, EMANATE.
750. Manipul-us, i, *bundle, wisp, troop.* Mantel-e, is, *towel*, (MANTLE). Manc-eps, ipis, *purchaser:* mancipi-um, i, *purchase, property, slave:* mancip-o, are, *I make over, sell:* emancip-o, are, *I set free*, EMANCIPATE. Mansuesc-o, ere, *I grow tame* or *gentle·* mansuet-us, a, um, *tame, mild:* mansuetud-o, inis, *gentleness.* Cominus, *hand to hand, close.* Eminus, *afar.*—1. Marin-us, a, um, MARINE, (MARINER). Maritim-us, a, um, MARITIME.—5. Mascul-us, a, um, masculin-us, a, um, MASCULINE. Marit-us, i, *husband;* marit-a, æ, *wife.*—6. Matern-us, a, um, *motherly*, MATERNAL. Matrimoni-um, i, MATRIMONY. Matron-a, æ, MATRON. —8. Maturit-as, atis, MATURITY. Matur-o, are, *I hasten.* Immatur-us, a, um, *unripe*, IMMATURE. Præmatur-us, a, um, PREMATURE.—9. Medic-us, a, um, *healing*, MEDICAL. Medicin-a, æ, MEDICINE. Medic-or, ari, *I heal.* Remedi-um, i, REMEDY.
760. Meditatio, nis, *practice*, MEDITATION. Præmedit-or, ari, I PREMEDITATE. Mediocris, *moderate:* mediocrit-as,

3. mel, lis, *honey*.
4. membr-um, i, *limb*, MEMBER.
5. memin-i, isse, I REMEMBER, (mens).
6. mend-a, æ, *error*.
7. mendic-us, i, *beggar*.
8. men-s, tis, MIND, *intellect*.
9. mens-a, æ, *table*.
770. mens-is, is, *month*.
1. ment-ior, iri, *I invent, speak falsely*, (mens).
2. me-o, are, *I go*.
3. mer-eo, ěre, *I earn*.
4. merg-o, ěre, *I dip*, MERGE.
5. mer-us, a, um, MERE, *pure, unmixed*.
6. mer-x, cis, *ware*.
7. metall-um, i, METAL, *mine*.
8. met-ior, iri, I MEASURE.
9. met-o, ěre, *I mow, reap*.
780. metu-s, us, *fear*.
1. me-us, a, um, MY, MINE.
2. mic-o, are, *I glitter, flicker*.

atis, MEDIOCRITY. Dimidi-us, a, um, *half.*—4. Membran-a, æ, *parchment*, MEMBRANE.—5. Memor, is, *mindful:* immemor, is, *unmindful:* memori-a, æ, MEMORY: memor-o, commemor-o, are, *I mention*, COMMEMORATE, (MEMORABLE).—6. Mendos-us, a, um, *faulty.* Emend-o, *I correct*, EMEND, AMEND.—7. Mendicit-as, atis, *beggary*, MENDICITY. Mendic-o, are, *I beg.*—8. Amen-s, demen-s, tis, *silly, mad:* amenti-a, dementi-a, æ, *folly, madness.* Comminisc-or, i, *I invent*, (COMMENT): comment-um, i, *invention;* comment-or, ari, *I meditate, compose.* Reminisc-or, i, *I remember.*
771. Mend-ax, acis, *lying*, MENDACIOUS: mendaci-um, i, *a lie.*—2. Comme-o, are, *I move from place to place:* commeat-us, us, *transport, furlough, provisions* (of an army). Per, re,-meo. Semit-a, æ, *path;* tram-es, itis, *path.*—3. Mer-eor, eri, *I deserve.* Merit-um, i, *desert*, MERIT. Merc-es, edis, *hire, pay, fee.* Com, de, e, pro,-mereo and eor.—4. Emerg-o, ere, *I rise out of*, EMERGE. De, im, sub,-mergo, (IMMERSE).—6. Merc-or, ari, *I traffic;* mercat-us, us, *traffic*, MART. Mercat-or, oris, MERCHANT. Commerci-um, i, COMMERCE.— 8. Mensur-a, æ, MEASURE. Immens-us, a, um, *immeasurable*, IMMENSE. Ad, com, de, di, e, per,-metior. Met-a, æ, *goal.*—9. Mess-is, is, *crop, harvest.* Mess-or, oris, *reaper, mower.* Demet-o, *I mow down.*
780. Metu-o, are, *I fear.*—2. Dimic-o, are, *I contend.* Emic-o,

3. migr-o, are, *I depart*, MIGRATE.
4. mille, *thousand*, (Num.) (MILLION).
5. min-æ, arum, *threats*.
6. minist-er, ri, *servant*, MINISTER.
7. min-or, us, *less*, (MINORITY).
8. mir-us, a, um, *wonderful*.
9. misc-eo, ĕre, *I mingle*, MIX.
790. miser, a, um, *wretched*.
1. mit-is, e, MILD.
2. mitr-a, æ, *turban*, MITRE.
3. mitt-o, ĕre, *I send*.

are, *I leap forth.*—3. Migratio, nis, MIGRATION. Emigr-o, are, I EMIGRATE. Com, de, im, re, trans,-migro.— 4. Mil-es, itis, *soldier :* militar-is, e, MILITARY : milit-o, are, *I serve as a soldier :* militi-a, æ, *warfare, war-service.*— 5. Min-ax, acis, *threatening.* Min-or, ari, *I threaten :* com, inter,-minor. Mineo, ere, (obs.) *I tower ;* emin-eo, *I tower,* (EMINENT) ; immin-eo, *I tower over, impend,* (IMMINENT) ; promin-eo, *I jut forward,* (PROMINENT). —6. Ministeri-um, i, *service.* Ministr-o, are, *I supply :* administr-o, are, *I supply to,* ADMINISTER.—7. Minim-us, a, um, *least.* Minu-o; com, de, di, im,-minu-o, ere, *I lessen,* DIMINISH : minut-us, a, um, *lessened, small,* MINUTE.— 8. Mir-or, admir-or, ari, *I wonder,* ADMIRE : mirabil-is, admirabil-is, e, *wonderful,* ADMIRABLE : miracul-um, i, MIRACLE, MARVEL. Nimirum, *namely, doubtless.*— 9. Mistur-a, æ, *mingling,* MIXTURE. Ad, com, im, inter, per,-misceo. Promiscu-us, a, um, PROMISCUOUS.
790. Miseri-a, æ, MISERY. Miser-et, *it pitieth,* (impers.) miser-eor, eri, miseresc-o, ere, miser-or, ari, commiser-or, ari, *I pity,* COMMISERATE : miserabil-is, e, *pitiable,* MISERABLE. Misericor-s, dis, *compassionate,* MERCIFUL : misericordi-a, æ, MERCY, *pity.*—1. Mitesc-o, ere, *I grow mild, soften.* Mitig-o, are, *I soften,* MITIGATE.—3. Miss-us, us ; missio, nis, *sending,* MISSION. Missil-is, e, MISSILE. Admitt-o, I ADMIT, *commit.* Amitt-o, *I lose,* (AMISS). Committ-o, *I join, entrust,* COMMIT : commiss-um, *trust,* COMMISSION, (COMMITTEE). Demitt-o, *I let down, send forth,* (DEMISE) : demiss-us, *cast down, humble.* Dimitt-o, *I send away,* DISMISS. Intermitt-o, I INTERMIT. Omitt-o, I OMIT, *leave off.* Permitt-o, ere, *I entrust,* PERMIT : permissi-o, nis, PERMISSION. Promitt-o, *I send forth,* PROMISE. Remitt-o, *I send back, slacken,* REMIT : remiss-us, a, um, *slackened,* REMISS. Submitt-o, *I set down, set under, lower, send secretly,* SUBMIT : submiss-us, a, um, SUBMISSIVE : submissio, nis, SUB-MISSION. Transmitt-o, I TRANSMIT. Also, e, im, intro,

4. mod-us, i, *measure, manner*, MODE.
5. mœr-eo, ēre, I MOURN.
6. mol-a, æ, MEAL, *cake*, MILL.
7. mol-es, is, *mass, dam*, MOLE.
8. moll-is, e, *soft*, (moveo).
9. mon-eo, ēre, *I advise, remind*, (mens).
800. mon-s, tis, MOUNTAIN.
1. monstr-o, are, *I show*, (moneo).
2. mor-a, æ, *delay*.
3. morb-us, i, *disease*, (MORBID).
4. mord-eo, ēre, *I bite*.
5. mor-s, tis, *death*.
6. mōs, mōris, *custom*, (MORAL).
7. mov-eo, ēre, I MOVE.

præ, præter,-mitto, (EMIT, EMISSARY, PREMISE, &c.) —4. Admodum, *very, much*. Modul-us, i, *measure*, MODEL: modul-or, ari, *I tune*, MODULATE. Modò, *just now, only*. Modic-us, a, um, *moderate, slight*. Moder-or, ari, *I rule, govern;* moderat-us, a, um, MODERATE: moderatio, nis, *government*, MODERATION. Modest-us, a, um, *moderate*, MODEST: modesti-a, æ, *moderation*, MODESTY. Commod-us, a, um, *convenient, advantageous*, COMMODIOUS: commod-um, i, *advantage:* incommodus, a, um, *inconvenient, disadvantageous:* incommod-um, i, *disadvantage:* commodit-as, atis, *convenience*, COMMODITY: commod-o, are, *I lend, suit:* accommod-o, are, *I suit*, ACCOMMODATE: commodùm, *in good time.*—5. Mœr-or, oris, *mourning*. Mœst-us, a, um, *sad:* mœstiti-a, æ, *sadness.*—6. Mol-o, ere, *I grind;* molit-or, oris, MILLER: emolument-um, i, *profit*, EMOLUMENT. Immol-o, are, *I sacrifice*, IMMOLATE.— 7. Molest-us, a, um, *troublesome, annoying:* molesti-a, æ, *annoyance*, (MOLEST). Mol-ior, iri, *I contrive, effect with trouble;* demol-ior, I DEMOLISH.—8. Molliti-a, æ, and es, ei, *softness, effeminacy*. Moll-io, emoll-io, ire, *I soften.*— 9. Monit-um, i, monitio, nis, *advice, warning:* monit-or, oris, *adviser*. Moniment-um, i, *memorial*, MONUMENT. Monet-a, æ, *coin*, MONEY. Admon-eo, ere, I ADMONISH. Also, com, præ, sub,-moneo.
801. Monstr-um, i, *prodigy*, MONSTER. Demonstro, *I point out, prove*, DEMONSTRATE. Also, com, præ,-monstro.— 2. Mor-or, ari, *I delay:* commor-or. ari, *I abide, reside.*— 4. Mord-ax, acis, *biting*. Mors-us, us, *bite.*—5. Mortal-is, e, MORTAL. Mor-ior, i, *I die.*—6. Moros-us, a, um, MOROSE. —7. Mobil-is, e, MOVEABLE. Mot-us, us, MOTION. Moment-um, i, *impulse, force*, MOMENT. Ad, a, com, de, di, e, per, pro, re, se, sub, trans,-moveo, (COMMOTION, EMOTION, PROMOTE, REMOVE, REMOTE, &c.)

8. mox, *by and by.*
9. mug-io, ire, *I low, bellow.*
810. mulc-eo, ēre, *I soothe.*
   1. mulct-a, or mult-a, æ, *fine,* MULCT.
   2. mulg-eo, ēre, I MILK.
   3. mulier, is, *woman.*
   4. mult-us, a, um, MUCH, *many.*
   5. mund-us, a, um, *clean.*
   6. mund-us, i, *world.*
   7. mun-us, eris, *gift, duty, office.*
   8. murmur, is, MURMUR.
   9. mur-us, i, *wall.*
820. mus, muris, MOUSE.
   1. mus-a, æ, MUSE, *song.*
   2. musc-a, æ, *fly.*
   3. musc-us, i, MOSS.
   4. mutil-us, a, um, MUTILATED.
   5. mut-o, are, *I change,* (moveo).
   6. mut-us, a, um, *dumb,* MUTE.
   7. myrt-us, i, MYRTLE-*tree.*
   8. Nam, namque, *for.*
   9. nancisc-or, i, *I acquire, find.*
830. nar-is, is, *nostril.*
   1. narr-o, are, *I relate,* (NARRATION).

---

812. Mulctr-a, æ, *milk-pail.*—3. Muliebr-is, e, *womanish, womanly.*
—4. Multitud-o, inis, MULTITUDE. Multifariàm, *in many places,* (MULTIFARIOUS). Multipl-ex, icis, *manifold.*—
5. Immund-us, a, um, *unclean.* Munditi-a, æ, *cleanliness, neatness.*—7. Muni-a, orum, *duties :* munic-eps, ipis, *burgess ;* municipi-um, i, *borough;* municipal-is, e, MUNICIPAL. Munific-us, a, um, MUNIFICENT : munificenti-a, æ, MUNIFICENCE. Commun-is, e, COMMON : communio, nis, COMMUNION : communic-o, are, *I impart,* COMMUNICATE. Immun-is, e, *exempt* (from burdens) : immunit-as, atis, IMMUNITY. Muner-o, or remuner-o, are, or, ari, *I present,* REMUNERATE.—8. Murmur-o, are, *I murmur.* Ad, re,-murmuro.—9. Mœni-a, orum, *city-walls :* Mun-io, ere, *I fortify, prepare :* muniment-um, i, *fortification,* (AMMUNITION). Circum, com, per, præ,-munio.
820. Muscipul-um, i, *mouse-trap.* Mustel-a, æ, *weasel.*—1. Music-us, a, um, MUSICAL. Music-a, æ, MUSIC.—5. Mutatio, nis, *change.* Mutabil-is, e, *changeable,* MUTABLE. Mutu-us, a, um, MUTUAL : mutu-or, ari, *I borrow.* Com, im, per, -muto.

D

2. nasc-or, i, *I am born.*
3. nas-us, i, NOSE.
4. nav-is, is, *ship*, (NAVY).
5. nĕ, *lest.*
6. nĕ, *whether?*
7. nebul-a, æ, *thin-cloud.*
8. necesse, *necessary*, (Def.)
9. nect-o, ĕre, *I twine, join.*
840. neg-o, are, *I deny, say not.*
1. nem-o, ĭnis, *nobody*, (ne-homo).
2. nempe, *to wit.*
3. nem-us, ŏris, *forest.*
4. nep-os, otis, *grandson.*
5. nequam, *wicked, worthless*, (Def.)
6. neque, nec, *nor, and not.*
7. nerv-us, i, *string*, NERVE.
8. nex, nĕcis, *death.*
9. nid-us, i, NEST.
850. nig-er, ra, rum, *black*, (NEGRO).
1. nihil, nihil-um, i, *nothing*, (ne hilum).
2. nimĭs, *too, too much.*
3. nisi, ni, *unless.*
4. nit-eo, ĕre, *I shine.*
5. nīt-or, i, *I lean, strive, rely.*

832. Nat-us, i, *son.* Natur-a, æ, NATURE: natural-is, e, NATURAL. Nativ-us, a, um, NATIVE. Natal-is, e, NATAL. Natio, nis, NATION. Cognat-us, i, *a relative.* Agnat-us, i, *a relative on the father's side.* Prognat-us, a, um, *descended from.* E, in, re,-nascor.—4. Naval-is, e, NAVAL. Navit-a, naut-a, æ, *sailor*, (NAUTICAL). Naufrag-us, a, um, *shipwrecked.* Naufragi-um, i, *shipwreck.* Navig-o, are, *I sail,* NAVIGATE. Nause-a, æ, *sea-sickness*, (NAUSEOUS). —5. Neve, neu, *and lest.* Nedum, *much less.* Nequidquam, *in vain.* Nequaquam, *by no means.*—8. Necessari-us, a, um, NECESSARY. Necessit-as, atis, NECESSITY, *intimacy.*— 9. Nex-us, us, *bond, union.* Connect-o, ere, *I join together,* CONNECT. An, in, sub,-necto, (ANNEX).

840 Negatio, nis, NEGATION. Deneg-o, are, I DENY. Ab, per, re,-nego, (RENEGADE).—4. Nept-is, is, *granddaughter.* Pronep-os, otis, *great-grandson.*—5. Nequiti-a, æ, *wickedness.* —7. Enerv-o, are, *I weaken,* ENERVATE.—8. Nec-o, are, *I kill.*

852. Nimi-us, a, um, *excessive.*—4. Nit-or, oris, *sheen.* Nitid-us, a, um, *shining, neat.* Nitesco, eniteo, enitesco.—5. Nis-us, us, *effort.* Obnit-or, renit-or, i, *I strive against.* Ad, con,

6. niv-eo, ĕre, *I wink*, (obs.)
7. nix, nivis, *snow.*
8. no, nare, *I swim.*
9. nobil-is, e, NOBLE, (nosco).
860. noc-eo, ēre, *I hurt.*
   1. nod-us, i, KNOT.
   2. nom-en, inis, NAME, (nosco).
   3. non, NOT.
   4. norm-a, æ. *rule.*
   5. nosc-o, ĕre, I KNOW.
   6. not-us, i, *south-wind.*
   7. novem, NINE.
   8. nov-us, a, um, NEW, *unprecedented.*
   9. nox, noctis, NIGHT.
870. nub-es, is, *cloud.*
   1. nub-o, ere, *I marry,* (used of the woman only).

e, in, sub,-nitor.—6. Conniv-eo, ere, *I wink,* CONNIVE.—
7. Nive-us, a, um, *snow-white.* Nival-is, e; nivoe-us, a, um,
snowy. Ning-it, ere, (Impers.) *it snows.*—8. Nat-o, are,
I swim. Ad, e, in, præ, trans,-no, or nato.—9. Nobilit-as,
atis, NOBILITY. Ignobil-is, e, IGNOBLE.
860. Nocu-us, nociv-us, a, um, *hurtful.* Nox-a, æ, *hurt, harm,
guilt, punishment:* noxi-us, a, um, *harmful,* NOXIOUS:
innoxi-us, a, um, *harmless,* INNOXIOUS: obnoxi-us, a, um,
liable, subject, OBNOXIOUS. Nocen-s, tis, *hurtful, guilty:*
innocen-s, tis, *harmless,* INNOCENT: innocenti-a, æ,
INNOCENCE.—2. Nomin-o, are, *I name,* NOMINATE:
denomin-o, I DENOMINATE. Prænomen, *a first name.*
Cognomen, *surname.* Agnomen, *added name.* Ignomini-a,
æ, IGNOMINY.—3. Nondum, *not yet.*—4. Enorm-is, e, *out
of rule,* (ENORMOUS). — 5. Not-a, æ, *mark,* NOTE:
not-o, are, *I mark, note, censure:* notabil-is, e, NOTABLE:
denot-o, are, *I mark out,* DENOTE. Notiti-a, æ, *knowledge:*
notesc-o, innotesc-o, ere, *I become known.* Notio, nis,
NOTION. Agnosco, *I know,* ACKNOWLEDGE. Cognosco,
I know, discover: cognitio, nis, *knowledge:* recognosco, I
RECOGNIZE. Ignosco, *I pardon.* Dignosco, *I distinguish.*
Not-us, a, um, *known;* ignot-us, a, um, *unknown.*—7. Nonus,
a, um, NINTH. Nundin-æ, arum, (for novendinæ) *a fair or
market held every nine days.*—8. Novit-as, atis, NOVELTY.
Nov-o, innov-o, are, *I make new,* INNOVATE: renovo, I
RENEW. Nuper, *lately.* Denuo, *anew.*—9. Nocturn-us, a,
um, *nightly.* Pern-ox, octis, *lasting all night:* pernoct-o, are,
I pass the night. Noctu-a, æ, *night owl.*
870. Nubil-us, a, um, *cloudy.*—1. Nupt-a, æ, *bride.* Nupti-æ,
arum, *wedding,* NUPTIALS. Connubi-um, i, *marriage.*

2. nud-us, a, um, *naked,* (NUDITY).
3. nug-æ, arum, *trifles.*
4. num, *whether?*
5. numer-us, i, NUMBER.
6. numm-us, i, *piece of money, sesterce.*
7. nunc, *now.*
8. nunquam, *never,* (ne-unquam).
9. nunti-us, i, *messenger.*
880. nu-o, ĕre, *I nod.*
1. nutr-io, ire, I NOURISH, (NUTRITIOUS).
2. nux, nŭcis, *walnut-tree.*
3. nymph-a, æ, NYMPH.
4. Ob, *on account of.*
5. obliqu-us, a, um, *slanting,* OBLIQUE.
6. oblivisc-or, i, *I forget.*
7. obscur-us, a, um, *dim,* OBSCURE.
8. occul-o, ĕre, *I hide,* (celo).
9. octo, EIGHT.
890. ocul-us, i, EYE.
1. od-i, isse, *I hate,* (Def.)
2. od-or, oris, *scent,* ODOUR.
3. offici-um, i, *duty,* OFFICE.
4. ole-a, æ, or oliv-a, æ, OLIVE-*tree.*

Innupt-us, a, um, *unmarried.* Pronub-a, æ, *bridesmaid.*—
2. Nud-o, denud-o, are, *I strip,* DENUDE.—3. Nug-or, ari, *I trifle:* nugat-or, oris, *trifler:* nugatori-us, a, um, *trifling,* NUGATORY. — 5. Numeros-us, a, um, NUMEROUS. Numer-o, are, *I reckon, count, pay;* innumerabil-is, e, INNUMERABLE: enumer-o, are, I ENUMERATE. An, di, per, re,-numero.— 9. Nunti-o, are, *I tell, announce:* annunti-o, I ANNOUNCE: denunti-o, *I declare,* DENOUNCE: denuntiatio, nis, *announcement,* DENUNCIATION: pronunti-o, I PRONOUNCE: renunti-o, *I report,* (RENOUNCE). Also, e, ob, præ,-nuntio.
880. Num-en, inis, *nod, Deity.* Nut-us, us, NOD. Nut-o, are, *I nod, totter.* Annu-o, ere, *I assent;* abnu-o, renu-o, *I refuse.* Innu-o, *I hint,* (INUENDO).—1. Nutriment-um, i, *nourishment,* NUTRIMENT. Nutr-ix, icis, NURSE.—2. Nucle-us, i, *kernel:* enucle-o, are, *I take out the kernel, explain.*— 6. Oblivio, nis, oblivi-um, i, *forgetfulness,* OBLIVION.— 7. Obscurit-as, atis, *darkness,* OBSCURITY. Obscur-o, are, *I darken, I obscure.*—8. Occult-us, a, um, *hidden,* OCCULT: occult-o, are, *I hide.*
891. Odi-um, i, *hatred:* odios-us, a, um, *hateful,* ODIOUS. — 2. Odor-o, are, *I scent:* odor-or, ari, *I smell out.*—

5.ᵃ ol-eo, ēre, *I grow*, (obs.)
5.ᵇ ol-eo, ēre, *I smell.*
6. olim, *once on a time, hereafter.*
7. om-en, inis, *presage*, OMEN.
8. omn-is, e, *all*, (OMNISCIENT, OMNIPRESENT, OMNIPOTENT, &c.)
9. on-us, eris, *burthen.*
900. opac-us, a, um, *shady, dark*, OPAQUE.
1. opin-or, ari, *I think.*
2. (ops) opis, *help*, (Def.)
3. oppid-um, i, *town.*
4. opt-o, are, *I wish.*
5.ᵃ op-us, eris, *work.*
5.ᵇ opus, *need*, (Def.)
6. or-a, æ, *border, shore.*
7. orb-is, is, *circle, world*, ORB.
8. orb-us, a, um, *bereft*, ORPHAN.
9. orc-us, i, *hell.*
910. ord-ior, iri, *I begin.*
1. ord-o, inis, ORDER, (DISORDER).

5.ᵃ Abol-eo, ere, I ABOLISH : abolesc-o, ere, *I decay.*
Adolesc-o, ere, *I grow to maturity;* adolescen-s, tis, *youth
or girl:* adult-us, a, um, *grown up*, ADULT. Exolesc-o, ere,
I decay. Inolesco, *I grow in:* indol-es, is, *natural disposition.*
Obsolesco, *I grow out of date:* obsolet-us, a, um, OBSOLETE.
Prol-es, is, *sprout, offspring.* Subolesco, *I grow under:*
sobol-es, is, *sucker, offspring.*—5.ᵇ Olfac-io, ere, *I smell:*
olfact-us, us, *smell.* Adol-eo, ere, *I burn* (incense): adolesc-o,
ere, *I am burning.* Redoleo, *I savour*, (REDOLENT).—
7. Omin-or, ari, *I forebode:* abomin-or, ari, *I deprecate,*
ABOMINATE.—8. Omnino, *utterly, in all.*—9. Onust-us,
a, um, *heavy-laden.* Oneros-us, a, um, *burthensome*, ONEROUS.
Oner-o, are, *I load:* exoner-o, are, *I unload*, EXONERATE.
900. Opac-o, are, *I darken.*—1. Opinio, nis, OPINION. Inopin-
us, a, um, *unexpected.*—2. Opim-us, a, um, *rich, splendid.*
Opulen-s, tis, *wealthy*, OPULENT. Opitul-or, ari, *I help.*
Inop-s, is, *destitute;* inopi-a, æ, *destitution.*—4. Optum-us, a,
um, *best.* Optio, nis, *choice*, OPTION. Adopt-o, are,
I ADOPT. Coopto, *I choose.* Exopto, *I earnestly desire.*
—5.ᵃ Opif-ex, icis, *workman.* Oper-a, æ, *exertion:* oper-æ,
arum, *workmen.* Oper-or, ari, *I work*, OPERATE, *sacrifice.*
—5.ᵇ Oport-et, ere, (Impers.) *it behoves.*—7. Orbit-a, æ, *wheel,*
ORBIT.—8. Orb-o, are, *I bereave:* orbit-as, atis, *childlessness.*
910. Exord-ior, *I commence:* exordi-um, i, *commencement.*—
1. Ordinari-us, a, um, ORDINARY: extraordinari-us, a,
um, EXTRAORDINARY. Ordin-o, are, *I arrange:*
D3

2. or-ior, iri, *I arise.*

3. orn-o, are, *I adorn.*

4. or-o, are, *I pray*, (os, oris).

5. os, oris, *mouth, countenance*, (ORAL).

6. os, ossis, *bone.*

7. osti-um, i, *mouth (of a river or harbour)*, (os).

8. ostre-a, æ, OYSTER.

9. oti-um, i, *leisure, retirement.*

920. ov-is, is, *sheep.*

1. ov-um, i, *egg*, (OVAL).

2. Pag-us, i, *village.*

3. palam, *openly.*

4. palat-um, i, *roof of the mouth*, PALATE.

5. pall-a, æ, *cloak*, PALL.

6. pall-eo, ēre, *I am* PALE.

7. palm-a, æ, PALM.

8. pal-us, ūdis, *marsh.*

9. pand-o, ĕre, *I spread.*

930. pang-o, ĕre, *I fasten.*

1. pan-is, is, *bread.*

2. papav-er, is, POPPY.

3. papilio, nis, *butterfly.*

inordinat-us, a, um, *unarranged*, INORDINATE.—2. Orig-o, inis, ORIGIN. Ad, co, ex, ob,-orior.—3. Ornat-us, us, ornament-um, i, ORNAMENT. Adorn-o, are, I ADORN. Suborn-o, are, I SUBORN.—4. Oratio, nis, *pleading, speech,* ORATION. Orat-or, oris, *pleader*, ORATOR. Oracul-um, i, ORACLE. Ador-o, I ADORE. Exor-o, *I beg off, intreat.* Peror-o, *plead through, finish a speech*, (PERORATION).— 6. Oscul-um, i, *kiss :* oscul-or, ari, *I kiss.*—8. Ostr-um, i, *purple dye.*—9. Otios-us, a, um, *leisurely.* Oti-or, ari, *I am at leisure.* Negoti-um, i, *business :* negoti-or, ari, *I trade,* NEGOTIATE.

920. Ovil-e, is, *sheepfold.* Ov-o, are, *I celebrate a victory* (by) Ovatio, nis, an OVATION (in which sheep were sacrificed). —2. Pagan-us, a, um, *belonging to a village*, PAGAN.— 5. Palli-um, i, *cloak.*—6. Pallid-us, a, um, PALE, PALLID. Pall-or, oris, PALENESS.—8. Palust-er, ris, re, *marshy.*— 9. Pass-us, us, *step*, PACE. Passim, *here and there, everywhere.* Expand-o, I EXPAND, (EXPANSE).

930. Pagin-a, æ, PAGE. Pal-a, æ, *shovel, bezil.* Pal-us, i, *stake,* PALE, (IMPALE). Comping-o, ere, *I fasten together,* (COMPACT): compag-es, is, *contexture.* Imping-o, ere, *I beat upon*, (IMPACT). Propag-o, inis, *progeny, offspring :* propag-o, are, I PROPAGATE. Repagul-um, i, *bolt.*—

4. par, is, *equal, like,* (PEER).

5. parc-o, ĕre, *I spare.*

6. par-eo, ēre, *I obey.*

7. pari-es, ĕtis, *wall (of a room).*

8. par-io, ĕre, *I bring forth.*

9. par-o, are, *I make ready.*

940. par-s, tis, PART.

1. parv-us, a, um, *little.*

2. pasc-o, ĕre, *I feed.*

3. passer, is, *sparrow.*

4. pat-eo, ēre, *I am open.*

5. pat-er, ris, FATHER.

6. pat-ior, i, *I suffer.*

7. patr-o, are, *I perform.*

8. pauc-us, a, um, *few.*

9. pavo, nis, *peacock.*

---

4. Pariter, *equally.* Par, is, PAIR. Compar-o, are, I COMPARE, (COMPARISON). Separ-o, are, I SEPARATE. Dispar, is, *unlike :* impar, is, *unequal.*—5. Parc-us, a, um, *thrifty :* parcimoni-a, æ, PARSIMONY.—6. Appar-eo, ere, I APPEAR : apparitio, nis, APPEARANCE, APPARITION. — 8. Paren-s, tis, PARENT. Part-us, us, *birth :* partur-io, ire, *I bring forth.*—9. Imper-o, are, *I command :* imperi-um, i, *command,* EMPIRE, (IMPERIAL). Apparo, *I get ready,* (APPARATUS). Comparo, *I procure.* Præparo, I PREPARE. Reparo, I REPAIR, *recover.*

940. Part-io, ire ; part-ior, iri, I *divide :* partitio, nis, PARTITION : impert-io, and ior, I IMPART. Partic-eps, ipis, *taking part, sharing :* particip-o, are, *I share,* PARTICIPATE. Partim, PARTLY. Portio, nis, PORTION : proportio, nis, PRO-PORTION. Exper-s, tis, *unsharing, free.*—1. Parum, *not much, too little :* parumper, *a little while.*—2. Past-us, us ; pastio, nis, *feeding,* PASTURE. Past-or, oris, *shepherd.* Pascu-a, orum, *pastures.* Pabul-um, i, *food.* Com, de,-pasco.—4. Patul-us, a, um, *open.*—5. Patern-us, a, um, *fatherly,* PATERNAL. Patri-a, æ, *country :* patri-us, a, um, *belonging to a father or country.* Patrimoni-um, i, PATRIMONY. Patrici-us, a, um, PATRICIAN. Patru-us, i, *uncle* (on father's side). Parricid-a, æ, a PARRICIDE : parricidi-um, i, PARRICIDE. Patron-us, i, PATRON : patrocini-um, i, PATRONAGE : patrocin-or, ari, I PATRONIZE.—6. Patien-s, tis, PATIENT : patienti-a, æ, PATIENCE. Passio, nis, *suffering,* (PASSION). Perpetior, *I endure.*—7. Impetr-o, are, *I obtain by asking.* Perpetr-o, are, I PERPETRATE.—8. Paucit-as, atis, *fewness,* PAUCITY. Paullum, paullulum. *very little ;* paullatim, *little by little ;* paullisper, *for a little while.*

950. pauper, is, (Adj.) POOR.
1. pa-x, cis, PEACE.
2. pecc-o, are, *I sin.*
3. pect-o, ĕre, *I comb.*
4. pect-us, oris, *breast.*
5.ᵃ pec-us, udis, ⎱ *cattle.*
5.ᵇ pec-us, ŏris, ⎰
6. pelag-us, i, *sea.*
7. pell-is, is, *skin.*
8. pell-o, ĕre, *I strike, drive away.*
9. pell-o, are, *I speak,* (obs.)
960. pend-eo, ēre, *I hang,* (PENDENT).
1. pend-o, ĕre, *I weigh, I pay.*
2. penn-a, æ, *wing, feather,* PEN.
3. penitus, *inly, deeply.*
4. per, *through, by.*
5. perd-ix, īcis, PARTRIDGE.
6. per-ior, iri, *I try,* (obs.)

950. Pauperi-es, ei, paupert-as, atis, POVERTY.—3. Pect-en,
inis, *comb.*— 5.ᵃ Pecuni-a, æ, *money,* (PECUNIARY).
Peculi-um, i, *private fund :* peculiar-is, e, PECULIAR :
pecul-or, ari, *I appropriate dishonestly,* PECULATE.—
8. Puls-us, us, *stroke,* PULSE. Puls-o, are, *I beat,*
(PULSATION). Appell-o, ere, *I put nigh, put to shore.*
Com, de, dis, ex, im, per, pro, re,-pello, (COMPEL, COM-
PULSION, DISPEL, EXPEL, IMPEL, IMPULSE,
PROPEL, REPEL, REPULSE, &c.)—9. Appell-o, are,
I call, APPEAL: appellatio, nis, APPEAL, APPELLATION.
Compell-o, are, *I address.* Interpell-o, are, *I interrupt.*
960. Pendul-us, a, um, *hanging,* (PENDULUM). Dependeo,
I hang from, DEPEND. Impendeo, *I hang over,* IMPEND.
Propendeo, *I lean forward ;* propens-us, a, um, *inclined :*
propensio, nis, *inclination,* PROPENSITY.—1. Pens-um, i,
task. Pensio, nis, *payment,* PENSION. Pens-o, are, *I
weigh :* compens-o, are, *I weigh with,* COMPENSATE.
dispens-o, are, *I disburse,* (DISPENSE): dispensat-or, oris,
steward. Pond-us, eris, *weight,* (PONDEROUS): ponder-o,
are, *I weigh,* (PONDER). Compendi-um, i, *abridgement,*
(COMPENDIOUS). Expend-o, ere, *I pay,* EXPEND.
Impendo, I SPEND: impendi-um, i; impens-a, æ; dispendi-
um, i, *cost.* Repend-o, ere, *I repay.* Suspend-o, ere, *I hang
up,* SUSPEND. Suspens-us, a, um, *hung up, wavering, in*
SUSPENSE. Ap, de, per,-pendo. — 3. Peuetr-o, are, I
PENETRATE. Penat-es, ium, *household gods.*—6. Perit-us,
a, um, *skilful.* Pericul-um, i, *danger,* PERIL. Pirat-a, æ,
PIRATE. Aper-io, ire, *I open.* Comper-io, ire, *I find.*

7. pes, pedis, FOOT.
8. pest-is, is, *plague*, PEST.
9. pet-o, ĕre, *I seek, sue.*
970. pig-er, ra, rum, *sluggish.*
1. pign-us, ŏris, *pledge.*
2. ping-o, ĕre, I PAINT.
3. pingu-is, e, *fat.*
4. pin-us, us, PINE-*tree.*
5. piper, is, PEPPER.
6. pir-us, i, PEAR-*tree.*
7. pisc-is, is, FISH.
8. pi-us, a, um, PIOUS, *dutiful.*
9. plac-eo, ēre, I PLEASE.
980. plant-a, æ, PLANT, *heel.*
1. plan-us, a, um, *level,* PLAIN.

Exper-ior, iri, *I try:* experienti-a, æ, EXPERIENCE.
Expert-us, a, um, EXPERIENCED, EXPERT: experiment-um, i, EXPERIMENT. Oper-io, ire, *I cover:* opper-ior, iri, *I await.* Reper-io, ire, *I find.*—7. Ped-es, itis, *on foot, foot-soldier:* peditat-us, us, *infantry.* Pedest-er, ris, re, *on foot,* PEDESTRIAN. Bip-es, edis, *two-footed,* BIPED. Quadrup-es, edis, *four-footed,* QUADRUPED. Exped-io, ire, *I disengage, forward:* expedit, *it is* EXPEDIENT: expeditio, nis, EXPEDITION. Imped-io, ire, *I entangle, hinder:* impediment-um, i, *hindrance,* IMPEDIMENT, *baggage.* Suppedit-o, are, *I supply.* Comp-es, edis, *fetter.*—8. Pestilen-s, tis, PESTILENT: pestilenti-a, æ, PESTILENCE. 9. Petitio, nis, *seeking, canvass,* PETITION. Petit-or, oris, *suer, candidate.* Petulan-s, tis, *freakish,* PETULANT. Appeto, *I desire;* appetit-us, us, APPETITE. Competo, I COMPETE, (COMPETENT, COMPETENCE). Expeto, *I seek, desire.* Impet-us, us, *rush, attack, ardour,* (IMPETUOUS). Perpetu-us, a, um, PERPETUAL. Repeto, *I reseek, reclaim,* REPEAT: repetitio, nis, REPETITION. Suppeto, *I supply.*
970. Pig-et, ere, (Impers.) *it irks.* Impig-er, ra, rum, *active.*—1. Pigner-o, oppigner-o, are, *I pawn.*—2. Pict-or, oris, *painter.* Pictur-a, æ, *painting,* PICTURE. Deping-o, I DEPICT.—6. Pir-um, i, PEAR. — 7. Piscat-or, oris, *fisherman.*—8. Piet-as, atis, *dutifulness,* PIETY. Pi-o, are, *I atone, propitiate;* expi-o, I EXPIATE. Impi-us, a, um, *undutiful,* IMPIOUS.—9. Placid-us, a, um, PLACID. Plac-o, are, *I propitiate, appease:* placabil-is, e, PLACABLE. Displic-eo, ere, I DISPLEASE. Compliceo, *I please,* (COMPLACENT, COMPLY, COMPLIMENT).
980. Plant-o, are, I PLANT: supplanto, I SUPPLANT.—1. Planè, PLAINLY, *quite.* Planiti-es, ei, *even ground.* Explan-o, are, I EXPLAIN: explanatio, nis, EXPLANATION.

2. plaud-o, ĕre, *I clap, applaud.*
3, pleb-s, is, *common people.*
4. plect-o, ere, *I bend.*
5. plen-us, a, um, *full,* (pleo).
6. pl-eo, ere, *I fill,* (obs.)
7. pler-ique, æque, aque, *most,* (plus).
8. plic-o, are, *I fold,* (PLAIT).
9. plor-o, are, *I lament.*
990. plum-a, æ, *feather,* PLUME.
1. plu-it, ĕre, *it rains,* (Impers.)
2. plus, pluris, (Adj.) *more,* (pleo).
3. pœn-a, æ, *punishment,* (PENAL).
4. poet-a, æ, POET.
5. pol-io, ire, I POLISH, (POLITE).
6. pomp-a, æ, *procession,* POMP.
7. pom-um, i, *apple.*
8. pone, *behind.*
9. pon-o, ĕre, *I place,* (POSITION).

2. Plaus-us, us, APPLAUSE. Plausibil-is, e, *deserving applause,* PLAUSIBLE. Plaustr-um, i, *waggon.* Applaud-o, ere, I APPLAUD. Explod-o, ere, *I hoot off,* EXPLODE. Supplod-o, *I stamp.*—3. Plebei-us, a, um, PLEBEIAN.— 4. Amplect-or, i, complect-or, i, *I embrace,* (COMPLEX). Perplex-us, a, um, *involved,* PERPLEXED. Plect-or, i, *I am punished.*—6. Suppl-eo, ere, I SUPPLY, *fill up :* supplement-um, i, SUPPLEMENT. Com, ex, im, op, re,-pleo, (COMPLETE, COMPLEMENT, EXPLETIVE, IMPLEMENT, REPLETE, &c.)—7. Plerumque, *generally.*—8. Applico, I APPLY. Complico, *I fold together,* (COMPLICATED). Explico, *I unfold, clear, explain,* (INEXPLICABLE). Implico, *I enfold, involve,* IMPLICATE, IMPLY. Replico, *I refold, unroll,* REPLY. Supplico, *I fold the knee,* SUPPLICATE: suppl-ex, icis, SUPPLIANT: supplici-um, i, *entreaty, punishment, execution.* Simpl-ex, icis, *without fold, straightforward,* SIMPLE : simplicit-as, atis, *candour,* SIMPLICITY. — 9. Comploro, *I bewail.* Deploro, I DEPLORE. Exploro, I EXPLORE, *test.* Imploro, I IMPLORE.
991. Pluvi-a, æ, *rain.* Pluvi-us, a, um, *rainy.*—2. Plurim-us, a, um, *most, very much.* — 3. Pœnit-et, ere, *it repenteth :* pœnitenti-a, æ, REPENTANCE, PENITENCE. Pun-io, ire, I PUNISH. Impun-is, e, *without punishment;* impunit-as, atis, IMPUNITY.—7. Pomari-um, i, *orchard.*—9. Appono, *I place by, serve up,* (APPOSITE). Compono, *I put together, arrange,* COMPOSE, (COMPOUND). Depono, *I lay down,* DEPOSE; deposit-um, i, DEPOSIT. Dispono, I DISPOSE,

1000. pon-s, tis, *bridge.*
  1. pŏpul-us, i, PEOPLE, (POPULOUS).
  2. pōpul-us, i, POPLAR-*tree.*
  3. porc-us, i, *pig,* (PORK).
  4. porro, *further.*
  5. port-a, æ, *gate,* (PORTER).
  6. port-o, are, *I carry.*
  7. port-us, us, *harbour,* PORT.
  8. posc-o, ĕre, *I demand.*
  9. post, *after.*
1010. post-is, is, *door*-POST.
  1. pot-is, e, *able.*
  2. pot-o, are, *I drink.*
  3. præ, *before.*
  4. præco, nis, *cryer, auctioneer.*
  5. præd-a, æ, PREY.
  6. præli-um, i, *battle.*

(DISPOSITION). Expono, I EXPOSE, *explain,* EX-POUND. Impono, *I lay on,* IMPOSE. Interpono, *I place between,* INTERPOSE. Oppono, *I place against,* OPPOSE; opposit-us, a, um, OPPOSITE. Postpono, *I put after,* POSTPONE. Præpono, *I set over, put before,* (PREPOSITION). Propono, *I put forward,* PROPOSE, (PROPOSITION). Repono, *I set apart, replace,* (REPOSE). Sepono, *I set aside.* Suppono, *I set under, substitute,* (SUPPOSE).

1000. Pontif-ex, icis, *chief priest,* PONTIFF.—1. Popular-is, e, POPULAR. Popul-or, depopul-or, ari, *I lay waste,* DEPOPULATE.—5. Portic-us, us, PORCH, PORTICO.—6. Ap, abs, com, de, ex, im, re, sup, trans,-porto, (COMPORT, DEPORTMENT, EXPORT, IMPORT, REPORT, SUPPORT, TRANSPORT, &c.) — 7. Importun-us, a, um, *inconvenient, annoying, harsh,* IMPORTUNATE: importunit-as, atis, IMPORTUNITY, *annoyance.* Opportun-us, a, um, *convenient,* OPPORTUNE: opportunit-as, atis, OPPORTUNITY.—8. Postul-o, are, *I demand:* expostulo, *I earnestly desire,* EXPOSTULATE. Ap, de, ex, re,-posco.—9. Poster-us, a, um, *hinder:* posterit-as, atis, POSTERITY.

1011. Poti-or, us, *preferable.* Poten-s, tis, *powerful,* POTENT, (POTENTATE): potenti-a, æ, potest-as, atis, POWER; impoten-s, tis, *powerless,* IMPOTENT. Pot-ior, iri, *I gain, enjoy.* Possum, posse, *I am able:* possibil-is, e, POSSIBLE.—2. Pot-us, us, potio, nis, potatio, nis, POTION, POTATION. Pot-or, oris, *drinker.* Pot-us, a, um, *drunk.* 3. Præter, *beside, except.* — 4. Præconi-um, i, *eulogy.*—5. Præd-or,

7. præmi-um, i, *prize.*
8. præ-s, dis, *surety.*
9. prandi-um, i, *breakfast, luncheon.*
1020. prat-um, i, *meadow.*
  1. prav-us, a, um, *vicious.*
  2. prehend-o, ĕre, *I take.*
  3. prem-o, ĕre, I PRESS, (PRESSURE).
  4. preti-um, i, PRICE, *value.*
  5. pre-x, cis, PRAYER, (Def.)
  6. pris, *formerly,* (obs.)
  7. priv-us, a, um, *individual, particular.*
  8. pro, *for.*
  9. probr-um, i, *disgrace.*
1030. prob-us, a, um, *virtuous.*
  1. procell-a, æ, *storm,* (cello).
  2. procer-us, a, um, *tall.*
  3. procul, *afar.*

ari, *I plunder.*—8. Prædi-um, i, *estate.*—9. Prand-eo, ere, *I breakfast, lunch :* imprans-us, a, um, *without breakfast.*
1021. Deprav-o, are, I DEPRAVE.—2. Prenso, are, *I grasp, canvass.* Apprehend-o, ere, *I lay hold on,* APPREHEND. Comprehend-o, ere, *I seize,* COMPRIZE, COMPREHEND, Deprehend-o, ere, *I detect.* Reprehend-o, ere, *I hold back. reprove,* REPREHEND.—3. Com, de, ex, im, op, re, sup,-primo, I COM—DE—EX—IM—OP—RE—SUP —PRESS.—4. Pretios-us, a, um, PRECIOUS.—5. Precari-us, a, um, *obtained by prayer,* PRECARIOUS. Prec-or, ari, I PRAY : deprec-or, ari, I DEPRECATE : imprec-or, ari, I IMPRECATE. Ap, com,-precor.—6. Prisc-us, a, um, *ancient.* Pristin-us, a, um, *former, ancient,* PRISTINE. Pridem, *erewhile.* Pri-ŏr, us, *former,* PRIOR. Prim-us, a, um, *first,* (PRIME, PRIMARY) : in-primis, apprimè, *eminently ;* primor-es, um, *first men ;* primordi-um, i, *first beginning :* princ-eps, ipis, *chief,* PRINCE : principi-um, i, *beginning,* PRINCIPLE : principal-is, e, PRINCIPAL : principat-us, us, *chief rank* or *power.* — 7. Priv-o, depriv-o, are, I DEPRIVE. Privat-us, a, um, PRIVATE. Privilegi-um, i, *special law,* PRIVILEGE.—8. Proin, proinde, *then, therefore, just as.* Protenus, *further, forthwith.* Prout, *according as.* Prorsus, *forward, entirely.*—9. Probros-us, a, um, *disgraceful.* Exprobr-o, are, *I reproach.* Opprobri-um, i, *disgrace, reproach,* (OPPROBRIOUS).
1030. Probit-as, atis, *honesty,* PROBITY. Prob-o, are, I PROVE, *commend :* probabil-is, e, *commendable,* PROBABLE : approbo, I APPROVE : approbatio, probatio, nis, PROOF, APPROBATION. Comprobo, *I prove :* improbo, reprobo,

4. proc-us, i, *suitor*.
5. prodigi-um, i, PRODIGY.
6. proficisc-or, i, *I set out*, (proficio).
7. prom-o, ĕre, *I draw out*, (pro-emo).
8. pron-us, a, um, *sloping down*, PRONE.
9. prope, *near*.
1040. proper-us, a, um, *hasty*, (prope).
1. propri-us, a, um, *peculiar*, *own*, PROPER, (prope).
2. propter, *near*, *on account of*, (prope).
3. prosper, a, um, *lucky*, PROSPEROUS.
4. pruden-s, (pro-videns), tis, (Adj.) PRUDENT.
5. public-us, a, um, PUBLIC, (pŏpulus).
6. pud-et, ĕre, *it shameth*, (Impers.)
7. puer, i, *boy*.
8. pugn-a, æ, *battle*.
9. pulch-er, ra, rum, *beautiful*.
1050. pul-vis, eris, *dust*.
1. pung-o, ĕre, *I prick*.
2. purpur-a, æ, PURPLE.
3. pur-us, a, um, PURE.
4. put-o, are, *I think*.

I disapprove, REPROVE. Improb-us, a, um, *dishonest*, *unjust*, *tiresome*. — 4. Proc-ax, acis, *wanton*, *bold*.— 7. Promt-us, a, um, *ready*, PROMPT. De, ex,-promo.— 9. Propi-or, us, *nearer*: proxim-us, a, um, *nearest*. Propinqu-us, a, um, *near*, *related*: propinquit-as, atis, *nearness*, PROPINQUITY. Propiti-us, a, um, PRO-PITIOUS.
1040. Proper-o, are, *I hasten*.—1. Propriet-as, atis, PROPERTY, PROPRIETY. — 3. Prosperit-as, atis, PROSPERITY. — 4. Prudenti-a, æ, PRUDENCE: impruden-s, tis, IMPRUDENT.— 5. Public-um, i, *tax*: publican-us, i, *taxgatherer*, PUBLICAN: public-o, are, *I confiscate*, (PUBLISH).—6. Pud-or, oris, *shame*, *modesty*. Pudic-us, a, um, *modest*, *chaste*. Impuden-s, tis, *shameless*, IMPUDENT. Repudi-um, i, *divorce*, (REPUDIATE).— 7. Puell-a, æ, *girl*. Pueril-is, e, *childish*, PUERILE. Pueriti-a, æ, *boyhood*.— 8. Pugn-o, are, *I fight*: pugn-ax, acis, *inclined to fight*, PUGNACIOUS: expugno, *I storm*: impugno, *I attack*, IMPUGN: propugno, *I fight for*, *defend*: repugno, *I resist* (REPUGNANT). De, op, -pugo. Pugil, is, *boxer*, PUGILIST. 9. Pulchritud-o, inis, *beauty*.
1051. Punct-um, i, *prick*, POINT (PUNCTUAL, PUNCTUATION). Compungo, *I prick* (COMPUNCTION). Expungo, I EXPUNGE. 3. Purg-o, are, *I cleanse*, PURGE.—4. Amput-

E

5. Quær-o, ĕre, *I seek.*
6. qualis, *of what sort* (QUALITY).
7. quando, *when.*
8. quant-us, a, um, *how great,* (QUANTITY).
9. quat-io, ĕre, *I shake.*
1060. quatuor, *four.*
1. que, *and.*
2. querc-us, us, *oak.*
3. quer-or, i, *I complain.*
4. qui, quæ, quod, *who, which.*
5. quidem, *indeed.*
6. qui-es, ētis, *rest,* QUIET.
7. quot, *how many.*
8. Rabi-es, ei, *madness, rage.*
9. racem-us, i, *cluster.*
1070. radi-us, i, RAY.
1. rad-ix, icis, ROOT, (RADICAL).

o, are, *I lop off,* AMPUTATE. Comput-o, are, *I reckon,* COMPUTE. Disput-o, are, *I argue,* DISPUTE. Imput-o, are, *I set down,* IMPUTE. 5. Quæst-us, us, *gain,* QUEST. Quæstio, nis, *inquiry,* QUESTION. Acquiro, I ACQUIRE. Conquiro, *I seek out.* Disquiro, *I seek about:* disquisitio, nis, DISQUISITION. Exquiro, *I seek out:* exquisit-us, a, um, *sought out,* EXQUISITE. Inquiro, I INQUIRE. Requiro, *I seek, lack, want,* REQUIRE (REQUISITE, REQUEST). An, per,-quiro. 7. Aliquando, *sometimes, sometime or other.* 8. Quantùm, quàm, *how much.* Aliquant-us, a, um, *some considerable.* Quanquam, quamvis, *although.* Quasi, *as if.* Quantul-us, a, um, *how little.* 9. Quass-o, are, concut-io, ere, *I shake* (CONCUSSION). Discut-io, ere, *I shake about* or *asunder* (DISCUSS, DISCUSSION). Percut-io, ere, *I strike* (PERCUSSION): repercut-io, *I reverberate.* De, ex, in, re,-cutio.

1060. Quadrat-us, a, um, SQUARE. 3. Querul-us, a, um, *complaining,* QUERULOUS. Querel-a, æ; querimoni-a, æ, quest-us, us, *complaint* (QUARREL). Conqueror, *I complain.* 4. Quia, *because;* quippe, *for.* Quod, *that, because:* quin, quominus, *but that.* Quare, quapropter, *wherefore.* Quatenus, *how far, as far as.* Quo, *whither:* quorsum, *how far:* quoad, *as far as, until.* Quondam, *formerly, at times.* [See pronouns derived from qui in the Latin Grammar.]—6. Quiesc-o, ere, *I rest* (QUIESCENT): quiet-us, a, um, QUIET. Acquiesco, *I rest in,* ACQUIESCE. Requi-es, etis, REST; re, con,-quiesco, *I rest.*—7. Quoties, *how often.*—8. Rabid-us, a, um, *mad,* RABID.
1070. Radi-o, are, *I glitter,* RADIATE, (RADIANT).—1. Eradic-o,

2. rad-o, ĕre, *I shave*, RASE, (RAZOR).
3. ram-us, i, *bough.*
4. ran-a, æ, *frog.*
5. rap-io, ĕre, *I seize, snatch,* RAVISH.
6. rar-us, a, um, *uncommon,* RARE.
7. rauc-us, a, um, *hoarse.*
8. recen-s, tis, *fresh,* RECENT.
9. reg-o, ĕre, *I rule.*
1080. religio, nis, RELIGION, (relego).
1. rem-us, i, *oar.*
2. r-eor, eri, *I think, reckon.*
3. rep-o, ĕre, I CREEP, (REPTILE).
4. res, rei, *thing, fact, estate,* (REAL, REALITY, &c.)
5. ret-e, is, *net.*
6. rid-eo, ēre, *I laugh.*
7. rig-o, are, *I bedew, water.*
8. rig-eo, ĕre, *I am stiff.*
9. rip-a, æ, *bank.*

are, I ERADICATE.—2. Rastr-um, i, *harrow,* RAKE. Erado, I ERASE. Ab, cor,-rado.—5. Rapid-us, a, um, *fleet,* RAPID. Rapin-a, æ, RAPINE. Rap-ax, acis, RAPACIOUS. Ar, cor, pro,-ripio, *I seize.* Ab, de, e, præ, -ripio, *I snatch away.* Diripio, *I plunder.* Surripio, *I steal away,* (SURREPTITIOUS).—9. Regio, nis, REGION. Regim-en, inis, *government.* Regul-a, æ, RULE, (REGULAR, REGULATE, &c.) Rect-us, a, um, *straight,* RIGHT. Rex, regis, *king:* regi-us, a, um, ROYAL: regal-is, e, REGAL: regn-um, i, *kingdom,* REIGN: regn-o, are, *I rule,* REIGN. Arrig-o, ere, *I prick up.* Corrigo, I CORRECT. Dirigo, I DIRECT. Erigo, I ERECT. Pergo, *I proceed.* Porrigo, *I stretch.* Surgo, consurgo, exsurgo, *I arise,* (SURGE, INSURGENT).

1081. Rem-ex, igis, ROWER: remig-o, are, *I row:* remigi-um, i, *bank of oars, rowing.* Birem-is, e, *two-oared:* trirem-is, e, *three-oared,* &c.—2. Rat-us, a, um, *reckoned, settled,* (RATE, RATIFY). Ratio, nis, REASON, *system, reckoning, regard,* &c. (RATIONAL).—3. Ar, cor, ir, ob, per, sur,-repo.—4. Respublica, reipublicæ, REPUBLIC, *commonwealth.* Rĕfert, *it matters,* (Impers.)—5. Reticul-um, i, *small net,* RETICULE. Irret-io, ire, *I ensnare.*—6. Ridicul-us, a, um, *laughable,* RIDICULOUS. Ris-us, us, *laughter, smile.* Derideo, I DERIDE: deris-us, us, DERISION. Ar, ir, sub,-rideo.—7. Rigu-us, a, um, *watered.* Irrigo, *I water,* IRRIGATE.—8. Rigid-us, a, um, *stiff,* RIGID. Rig-or, oris, *stiffness,* RIGOUR.

1090. rit-us, us, RITE.
 1. riv-us, i, *stream*, RIVER.
 2. rix-a, æ, *quarrel*.
 3. rob-ur, oris, *oak, strength*.
 4. rod-o, ĕre, *I gnaw*.
 5. rog-o, are, *I ask*.
 6. ros, roris, *dew*.
 7. ros-a, æ, ROSE.
 8. rot-a, æ, *wheel*.
 9. rub-er, ra, rum, *red* (RUBY).
1100. rud-is, e, *untrained*, RUDE.
 1. rud-o, ĕre, *I bray*.
 2. ruf-us, a, um, *red-haired*.
 3. rug-a, æ, *wrinkle*.
 4. rug-io, ire, I ROAR.
 5. rumin-or, ari, *I chew the cud*, RUMINATE.
 6. rum-or, oris, *report*, RUMOUR.
 7. rump-o, ĕre, *I break*, (RUPTURE).
 8. ru-o, ĕre, I RUSH, *I fall*.
 9. rup-es, is, *crag* (rumpo).

1090. Ritè, *duly*.—1. Rivul-us, i, RIVULET. Rival-is, is, RIVAL. Deriv-o, are, *I draw away* (as water from a stream by a channel), DERIVE.—2. Rix-or, ari, *I wrangle*.—3. Robor-o, corrobor-o, are, *I strengthen*, CORROBORATE.—3. Robust-us, a, um, *stout*, ROBUST. — 4. Rostr-um, i, *beak*. Corrodo, I CORRODE. Ar, de, circum, præ,-rodo.—5. Rogatio, nis, *request, proposal, bill*. Abrogo, I ABROGATE. Arrogo, *I claim*, ARROGATE : arrogan-s, tis, ARROGANT : arroganti-a, æ, ARROGANCE. Interrogo, *I question*, INTERROGATE. Prorogo, I PROROGUE. Cor, de, e, ir, ob, per, sur,-rogo (DEROGATE, PREROGATIVE, &c.).—6. Roscid-us, a, um, *dewy*.—8. Rotund-us, a, um, ROUND. Rot-o, are, *I wheel* (ROTATION, ROTATORY).—9. Rubric-a, æ, *red ochre*, RUBRIC. Rub-eo, ere, rubesc-o, erubesc-o, ere, *I turn red, blush*. Rub-or, oris, *redness, blush*.
1100. Rudiment-um, i, RUDIMENT. Erud-io, ire, *I instruct, train :* erudit-us, a, um, *instructed*, ERUDITE.—1. Ruden-s, tis, *cable*.—7. Abrumpo, *I break off* (ABRUPT). Corrumpo, I CORRUPT. Erumpo, *I break out* (ERUP-TION). Interrumpo, *I break off*, INTERRUPT. Irrumpo, *I break in* (IRRUPTION). Dis, per, præ, pro,-rumpo.—8. Ruin-a, æ, *fall*, RUIN. Corruo, *I fall in*. Diruo, proruo, *I destroy*. Eruo, *I rout out*. Irruo, *I rush in*, Obruo, *I overwhelm*. Subruo, *I undermine*.

1110. rus, ruris, *country* (RURAL).
  1. rutil-us, a, um, *fiery-red.*
  2. Sacc-us, i, SACK.
  3. sac-er, ra, rum, SACRED.
  4. sæpĕ, *often.*
  5. sæv-us, a, um, *cruel,* SAVAGE.
  6. sag-io, ire, *I notice,* (SAGE) (obs.).
  7. sagitt-a, æ, *arrow.*
  8. sal, is, SALT, (SALINE).
  9. sal-io, ire, *I leap, I dance.*
1120. sal-ix, ĭcis, *willow.*
  1. salv-us, a, um, SAFE, *well,* (SALVATION).
  2. sanc-io, ire, *I establish, ratify.*
  3. sangu-is, ĭnis, *blood.*
  4. san-us, a, um, SOUND, *healthy,* SANE.
  5. sap-io, ĕre, *I taste, I am wise* (INSIPID).

1110. Rustic-us, a, um, RUSTIC.—1. Rutil-o, are, *I glitter.*—3. Sacr-o, consecr-o, are, I CONSECRATE : sacrament-um, i, *military oath* (SACRAMENT) : Execr-or, ari, *I curse,* EXECRATE : obsecr-o, are, *I beseech.* Sacerd-os, otis, *priest* (SACERDOTAL) : sacerdoti-um, i, *priesthood.* Sacrific-o, are, I SACRIFICE : sacr-um, i ; sacrifici-um, i, *sacrifice.* Sacrileg-us, a, um, SACRILEGIOUS : sacrilegi-um, i, SACRILEGE.—5. Sæviti-a, æ, *cruelty.* Sæv-io, de, ex,-sæv-io, ire, *I rage.*—6. Præsag-us, a, um, *foreboding :* præsag-io, ire, *I forebode :* præsagi-um, i, PRESAGE. Sag-ax, acis, SAGACIOUS : sagacit-as, atis, SAGACITY.—8. Salin-um, i, *salt-cellar.* Sal-es, ium, *wit.* Sal-um, i, *brine, sea.* Sals-us, a, um, *salt, witty :* insuls-us, a, um, *insipid, stupid.*—9. Salt-us, us, *leap, dance, glade.* As, de, dis, ex, in, præ, pro, re, tran,-silio. Salt-o, are, *I dance :* exsulto, *I bound,* EXULT : insulto, *I dance on,* INSULT : resulto, *I spring back, reecho* (RESULT).

1121. Sal-us, utis, *safety, health :* salutar-is, e, *wholesome,* SALUTARY. Salut-o, con,-salut-o, are, *I wish health,* SALUTE : salutatio, nis, SALUTATION. Salub-er, ris, re, *healthful,* SALUBRIOUS.—2. Sanctio, nis, SANCTION. Sanct-us, a, um, *sanctioned, holy,* (SAINT) : sanctit-as, atis, SANCTITY. — 3. Sanguine-us, a, um, *bloody,* (SANGUINE). Sanguinari-us, a, um, SANGUINARY. Consanguine-us, a, um, *related in blood :* consanguinit-as, atis, *blood-relationship,* CONSANGUINITY.—4. Sanè, *truly.* Sanit-as, atis, *health, soundness,* SANITY. San-o, are, *I cure :* consanesc-o, ere, *I get well.* Insan-us, a, um, *unsound, mad,* INSANE : insani-a, æ, *madness :* insan-io, ire, *I am mad.*—5. Sapien-s, tis, *wise ;* sapienti-a, æ,

E3

6. sarc-io, ire, *I darn*, *I patch*.
7. satis, *enough*.
8. sax-um, i, *stone*.
9. scand-o, ĕre, *I climb*.
1130. scel-us, eris, *crime*.
1. scen-a, æ, *stage*, SCENE.
2. schol-a, æ, SCHOOL, (SCHOLAR).
3. scind-o, ĕre, *I cut*, *tear*, (SCISSARS).
4. scintill-a, æ, *spark*, (scindo).
5. sc-io, ire, *I know*.
6. scopul-us, i, *rock*.
7. scrib-o, ĕre, *I write*, (SCRIBBLE).
8. scrupul-us, i, *pebble*, SCRUPLE, (SCRU-
   PULOUS).
9. scrut-or, ari, *I search*, (SCRUTINY, SCRU-
   TINIZE.)

wisdom. Sap-or, oris, SAVOUR.—6. Sart-or, oris, *cobbler*. Sarcin-a, æ, *burthen*, *pack*. Resarcio, *I patch up*.—7. Satiet-as, atis, SATIETY. Satur, a, um, *full*, *glutted*. Satir-a, æ, SATIRE. Sati-o, exsati-o, satur-o, exsatur-o, are, I SATIATE, SATURATE, *glut*. Satisdo, satisfacio, *I give security*, SATISFY, (SATISFACTION).—9. Scal-æ, arum, *stairs*, (SCALE). Adscendo, conscendo, *I climb*, ASCEND. Descendo, I DESCEND.
1130. Scelest-us, scelerat-us, a, um, *wicked*, *criminal*.—3. Sched-a, æ, *a leaf of paper*, (SCHEDULE). Ab, con, di, ex, per, pro, re,-scindo, (RESCIND).—5. Scien-s, tis; scit-us, a, um, *skilful*, *judicious*: inscien-s, tis, inscit-us, a, um, *unskilful*, *ignorant*, *injudicious*: scienti-a, æ, *knowledge*, SCIENCE, (SCIENTIFIC): inscienti-a, æ, insciti-a, æ, *ignorance*: sciscit-or, ari, *I inquire*: adscisc-o, ere, *I assume*, *choose*: conscisco, *I resolve*: descisco, *I revolt*: rescisco, *I obtain information*. Conscio, *I am conscious*: consci-us, a, um, *accomplice*, CONSCIOUS: conscienti-a, æ, co-knowledge, CONSCIENCE, *consciousness*. Insci-us, a, um, nesci-us, a, um, *unknowing*, *ignorant*: nescio, *I know not*. Præscio, *I know beforehand*, (PRESCIENCE). Scilicet, *to wit*.—7. Scrib-a, æ, *secretary*, *notary*, SCRIBE. Script-um, i, scriptio, nis, scriptur-a, æ, *writing*, SCRIPTURE. Script-or, oris, *writer*. Adscribo, *I enroll*, ASCRIBE. Conscribo, *I compose*, *levy*. Describo, *I mark out*, DESCRIBE: descriptio, nis, DESCRIPTION. Perscribo, *I write out*, *pay*. Præscribo, I PRESCRIBE: præscriptio, nis, PRESCRIPTION. Proscribo, I PROSCRIBE. Rescribo, *I write back*. Subscribo, *I write under*, SUBSCRIBE. Circum, tran,-scribo, I CIRCUM—TRAN—SCRIBE, (TRANSCRIPT).

1140. sculp-o, ĕre, *I engrave.*
  1. sec-o, are, *I cut* (SEGMENT).
  2. secul-um, i, *generation.*
  3. sed, *but.*
  4. sed-eo, ēre, I SIT.
  5. sedul-us, a, um, *diligent*, SEDULOUS (sedes).
  6. segn-is, e, *lazy, slothful.*
  7. semel, *once.*
  8. semis, *half.*
  9. semper, *always.*
1150. sen-ex, is, *old.*
  1. sent-io, ire, *I feel, think, perceive* (SENTIMENT).
  2. sepel-io, ire, *I bury.*

1140. Sculpt-or, oris, *engraver*, SCULPTOR. Sculptur-a, æ, SCULPTURE. Ex, in,-sculpo.—1. Secur-is, is, *axe.* Sectio, nis, *cutting, confiscation* (SECTION). Reseco, *I cut off, pierce.* De, ex, præ, pro, sub,-seco (DISSECT).— 2. Secular-is, e, SECULAR.—4. Sed-es, is, SEAT. Sell-a, æ, *seat;* subselli-um, i, *bench.* Sessio, nis, *sitting,* SESSION. Sid-o, ere, *I sink, settle, sit:* subsido, *I sink down,* SUBSIDE: as, con, de, in, re,-sido. Assideo, *I sit by:* assidu-us, a, um, *persevering,* ASSIDUOUS. Desideo, *I lounge:* des-es, idis, *slothful:* desidi-a, æ, *sloth.* Dissideo, *I differ:* dissidi-um, i, *dissension.* Insideo, *I sit on, beset:* insidi-æ, arum, *ambush, plot, hostile design:* insidios-us, a, um, *treacherous,* INSIDIOUS: insidi-or, ari, *I plot against.* Obsideo, *I blockade, besiege;* obsidio, nis, obsidi-um, i, *siege:* obs-es, idis, *hostage.* Possideo, I POSSESS: possessio, nis, POSSESSION. Præsideo, I PRESIDE: præs-es, idis, PRESIDENT: præsidi-um, i, *garrison, protection.* Resideo, I RESIDE, *settle, sink:* residu-us, a, um, *remaining* (RESIDUE): res-es, idis, *lingering, drooping.* Subsideo, *I stay:* subsidi-um, i, *reserve, support:* subsidiari-us, a, um, SUBSIDIARY. Supersedeo, *I dispense with,* SUPERSEDE. Sed-o, are, *I calm, allay* (SEDATE).—6. Segniti-a, æ; es, ei; *sloth, laziness.*—8. Semide-us, i, *demigod.* Semivir, *half-man.* Semicircul-us, i, SEMICIRLE. Semisepult-us, a, um, *half buried, &c., &c.* Sesterti-us, i, SESTERCE.

1150. Senil-is, e, *aged.* Senesc-o, consenesc-o, ere, *I·grow old.* Seni-um, i, *senect-us, utis, senect-a, æ, *old age.* Senat-us, us, SENATE: senat-or, oris, SENATOR.—1. Sententi-a, æ, *opinion,* SENTENCE. Sens-us, us, *feeling,* SENSE, (SENSIBLE, SENSITIVE). Sensim, *gradually.* Assentio, assentior, I ASSENT: assent-or, ari, *I flatter.* Consentio, *I agree,* CONSENT: consentane-us, a, um, *agreeing, suitable.* Dissentio, *I differ,* DISSENT. dissensio, nis, DISSENSION. Per, præ, sub,-sentio. 2. Sepultur-a, æ, *burial,* SEPULTURE.

3. sep-es, is, *hedge*.
4. septem, SEVEN.
5. sequ-or, i, *I follow* (SEQUEL).
6. seren-us, a, um, SERENE.
7. seri-us, a, um, SERIOUS.
8.ᵃ ser-o, ĕre, I SOW.
8.ᵇ ser-o, ĕre, *I join*.
9. serp-o, ĕre, *I crawl*.
1160. serr-a, æ, *saw*.
1. serv-us, i, *slave*, SERVANT.
2. serv-o, are, I PRESERVE.
3. ser-us, a, um, *late*.
4. sever-us, a, um, *stern, strict*, SEVERE.
5. sex, SIX.
6. sex-us, us, SEX.

Sepulcr-um, i, *tomb*, SEPULCRE.—3. Sep-io, ire, *I hedge, fence*: sept-um, i, *inclosure*: circum, inter, ob, præ,-sepio. Præsep-e, is, *stable, manger*.—5. Secund-us, a, um, *following*, SECOND, *propitious*: secund-o, are, *I favour*, SECOND: secundum, *following next to, according to*. Sect-a, æ, SECT. Sect-or, ari, *I follow*: insector, *I assail, persecute*: as, con,-sector. Assequor, *I attain*. Consequor, *I follow, attain* (CONSEQUENCE). Exsequor, *I follow out*, EXECUTE: exsequi-æ, arum, *funeral train*. Insequor, *I follow up*, ENSUE. Obsequor, *I obey*: obsequi-um, i, *obedience, flattery* (OBSEQUIOUS). Persequor, I PURSUE, PERSECUTE. Prosequor, *I attend, follow*, PROSECUTE. Subsequor, *I follow behind* (SUBSEQUENT).—8.ᵃ Seg-es, etis, *crop*. Sem-en, inis, SEED: seminari-um, i, SEMINARY: semin-o, are, *I sow*: dissemin-o, *I scatter*, DISSEMINATE. Sat-or, oris, *sower*, SIRE. Insero, *I ingraft*. Con, ob,-sero: obsit-us, a, um, *covered, beset*—8.ᵇ Ser-a, æ, *bolt*. Seri-es, ei, SERIES. Sermo, nis, *conversation, discourse*, SERMON. Sert-um, i, *wreath*. Assero, I ASSERT. Consero, *I join*. Desero, I DESERT. Dissero, *I argue* (DISSERTATION). Insero, I INSERT. Præsertim, *especially*. Exsero, I EXERT, *put forth*.—9. Serpen-s, tis, SERPENT.
1161. Servil-is, e, *slavish*, SERVILE. Serviti-um, i, servit-us, utis, *slavery*, SERVITUDE. Serv-io, ire, *I am a slave*, I SERVE. As, in, de, sub,-servio, (SUBSERVIENT).—2. Observo, *I watch, court*, OBSERVE: observatio, nis, OBSERVATION. Reservo, I RESERVE. As, con, -servo.—4. Assever-o, are, *I declare*: asseveratio, nis, ASSEVERATION. Persever-o, are, I PERSEVERE: perseveranti-a, æ, PERSEVERANCE. Severit-as, atis,

7. si, *if*.
8. sibil-us, i, *hiss*.
9. sic, *thus, so*.
1170. sicc-us, a, um, *dry*.
1. sid-us, eris, *constellation, star*.
2. sign-um, i, SIGN, *standard*.
3. sil-eo, ēre, *I am* SILENT.
4. silv-a, æ, *wood, forest*, (SYLVAN).
5. simil-is, e, *like*, SIMILAR, (SEMBLANCE, RESEMBLE).
6. simpl-ex, ĭcis, (Adj.) SIMPLE, (plico).
7. sincer-us, a, um, *pure*, SINCERE.
8. sine, *without*.
9. singul-i, æ, a, *each*, SINGLE.
1180. singult-us, us, *sob*.
1. sinist-er, ra, rum, *left, unlucky*, SINISTER.
2. sin-o, ĕre, *I leave, allow*.
3. sin-us, us, *fold, curvature*.
4. sip-o, are, *I throw*, (obs.)
5. sist-o, ĕre, *I stop*.

strictness, SEVERITY.—8. Sibil-o, are, *I hiss*.—9. Sicut, *as*.
1170. Sicc-o, desicc-o, exsicc-o, are, *I dry up*.—1. Sidere-us, a, um, *starry*. Consider-o, are, I CONSIDER. Desider-o, are, *I regret*, DESIRE: desideri-um, i, *regret*, DESIRE. —2. Sigill-um, i, SEAL. Signific-o, are, *I make sign*, SIGNIFY. Sign-o, are, I SIGN, *mark out, seal :* assigno, I ASSIGN : consigno, *I seal*, CONSIGN. Designo, *I mark out*, DESIGN, DESIGNATE. Obsigno, *I seal up*. Resigno, *I unseal*, RESIGN. Ex, sub,-signo. Insign-is, e, *distinguished, remarkable :* insign-e, ia, ENSIGN : insign-io, ire, *I distinguish*.—3. Silenti-um, i, SILENCE. —5. Simul, *at the same time, together*. Similitud-o, inis, *likeness*, SIMILITUDE. Simul-o, are, *I liken, feign :* simulacr-um, i, *image :* simult-as, atis, *enmity :* dissimul-o, are, I DISSEMBLE. Assimil-is, consimil-is, e, *like :* assimil-o, are, I ASSIMILATE. Dissimil-is, e, *unlike*, DISSIMILAR.—9. Singular-is, e, *unparalleled*, SINGULAR.
1182. Sit-us, us, SITE, SITUATION. Desino, *I cease*.— 3. Sinu-o, are, *I wind :* insinuo, *I wind in*, INSINUATE. Sinuos-us, a, um, *winding*, SINUOUS.—4. Dissip-o, are, *I scatter, squander*, DISSIPATE.—5. Assist-o, *I stand by*, (ASSIST). Consist-o, *I halt, stop, rest*, CONSIST. Desisto, I DESIST. Existo, *I arise*, EXIST. Insisto, *I stand upon*, INSIST. Obsisto, *I oppose :* obstetr-ix, icis, *midwife*. Persisto, I PERSIST. Resisto, *I stop, stand still*, RESIST. Subsisto, *I halt*, SUBSIST. Absisto, *I*

6. sit-is, is, *thirst.*

7. sobri-us, a, um, SOBER, (se-ebrius).

8. soci-us, a, um, *allied, accompanying, partner.*

9. sol, is, *sun.*

1190. sol-eo, ēre, *I am wont.*

1. solid-us, a, um, SOLID, (solum).

2. sol-or, ari, *I comfort.*

3. sol-um, i, SOIL, *ground.*

4. solv-o, ĕre, *I loose, pay,* SOLVE (INSOLVENT).

5.ᵃ sol-us, a, um, *alone,* SOLE.

5.ᵇ sol-us, or soll-us, a, um, *entire* (obs.).

6. somn-us, i, *sleep.*

7. son-us, i, SOUND.

8. sop-or, oris, *slumber* (SOPORIFIC).

9. sorb-eo, ēre, *I suck in.*

depart, abstain.—6. Sit-io, ire, *I thirst.*—7. Sobriet-as, atis, SOBRIETY.—8. Social-is, e, SOCIAL. Societ-as, atis, *alliance, partnership,* SOCIETY. Sociabil-is, e, SOCIABLE. Soci-o, associ-o, consoci-o, are, *I ally,* ASSOCIATE: dissoci-o, are, *I dissever,* DISSOCIATE.—9. Solar-is, e, SOLAR. Solstiti-um, i, SOLSTICE.

1190. Insolen-s, tis, *unwonted,* INSOLENT: insolenti-a, æ, *inacquaintance,* INSOLENCE.—1. Solid-o, consolid-o, are, *I establish,* CONSOLIDATE.—2. Consol-or, ari, *I comfort,* CONSOLE. Solati-um, i, consolatio, nis, SOLACE, CONSOLATION, (INCONSOLABLE, DISCONSOLATE). —3. Exsul, is, *banished:* exsul-o, are *I am banished:* exsili-um, i, *banishment,* EXILE.—4. Solutio, nis, *loosing, payment,* SOLUTION. Absolvo, *I acquit,* ABSOLVE: absolutio, nis, *acquittal,* ABSOLUTION. Dissolvo, *I break up,* DISSOLVE: dissolut-us, a, um, DISSOLUTE: dissolutio, nis, DISSOLUTION. Exsolvo, *I release, perform, pay.* Persolvo, *I pay.* Resolvo, *I relax, melt,* RESOLVE (RESOLUTE, RESOLUTION).—5.ᵃ Solitud-o, inis, SOLITUDE. Solitari-us, a, um, SOLITARY. Desol-o, are, *I make lonely:* desolat-us, a, um, DESOLATE.— 5.ᵇ Soller-s, tis, *skilful, ingenious.* Sollerti-a, æ, *skill, diligence.* Sollemn-is, e, *annual,* SOLEMN. Sollicit-us, a, um, *anxious,* SOLICITOUS: sollicitud-o, inis, *anxiety,* SOLICITUDE : sollicit-o, *I make anxious, disturb,* (SOLICIT).—6. Somni-um, i, insomni-um, i, *dream.* Somni-o, are, *I dream.* Insomn-is, e, *sleepless.*—7. Son-o, are, *I sound;* circum, con, per, re,-sono (CONSONANT, RESOUND): sonit-us, us, *sound:* persŏn-a, æ, *mask, character,* PERSON. Disson-us, a, um, DISSONANT.—8. Sop-io, ire, *I lull.*—9. Absorbeo, I ABSORB. Ex, re,-sorbeo.

1200. sord-es, ium, *filth, meanness.*
  1. sor-or, oris, *sister.*
  2. sor-s, tis, *lot* (SORT).
  3. sosp-es, itis, *safe.*
  4. sparg-o, ĕre, *I scatter, sprinkle.*
  5. spati-um, i, SPACE, *distance.*
  6. spec-io, ĕre, I ESPY (obs.).
  7. spec-us, us, *cave.*
  8. spern-o, ere, *I despise,* SPURN.
  9. sp-es, ei, *hope.*
1210. spic-a, æ, *ear of corn,* SPIKE.
  1. spin-a, æ, *thorn,* SPINE.
  2. spir-o, are, *I breathe.*
  3. spiss-us, a, um, *thick, coagulated.*
  4. splend-eo, ĕre, *I glitter.*
  5. spoli-um, i, SPOIL.
  6. spond-eo, ĕre. *I betroth, I promise.*

1200. Sordid-us, a, um, *dirty, meanly clad,* SORDID. Sord-eo, ere, sordesc-o, ere, *I am dirty, I am cheap.*—2. Sort-ior, iri, *I receive by lot, I allot.* Consor-s, tis, *partner* (CONSORT). Exsor-s, tis, *unallotted.*—4. Ad, con, dis, in, re,-spergo (ASPERSE, DISPERSE, INSPERSION, &c.). 5. Spatios-us, a, um, SPACIOUS. Spati-or, ari, exspati-or, *I walk about,* EXPATIATE.—6. Speci-es, ei, *appearance, beauty, kind,* (SPECIAL): specios-us, a, um, *handsome,* SPECIOUS. Specim-en, inis, *sample, pattern,* SPECIMEN. Specul-a, æ, *watch-station.* Specul-or, ari, *I view, spy,* SPECULATE. Specul-um, i, *mirror.* Spect-o, are, *I behold :* spectat-or, oris, SPECTATOR: exspecto, *I await,* EXPECT: ad, de, in, pro, re, su,-specto. Adspic-io, ere, *I behold :* adspect-us, us, *view,* ASPECT. Conspicio, *I view :* conspic-or, ari, *I view.* Despicio, *I look down on,* DESPISE. Inspicio, *I look into,* INSPECT. Perspicio, *I see through, understand :* perspic-ax, acis, PERSPICACIOUS. Prospicio, *I look forward :* prospect-us, us, PROSPECT. Respicio, *I look back on, regard :* respect-us, us, *regard,* RETROSPECT, RESPECT. Suspicio, *I look up to :* suspic-or, ari, I SUSPECT: suspicio, nis, SUSPICION.—7. Spelunc-a, æ, *cavern.*—8. Adspern-or, ari, *I reject, spurn.*—9. Sper-o, are, *I hope :* despero, I DESPAIR.

1210. Spicul-um, i, *point, dart.*—2. Spirit-us, us, *breath,* SPIRIT. Suspiro, *I sigh :* suspiri-um, i, *sigh.* Ad, con, ex, in, re,-spiro, I A-CON-EX-IN-RE-SPIRE.—4. Splendid-us, a, um, *bright,* SPLENDID. Splend-or, oris, *brilliancy,* SPLENDOUR. Splendesc-o, ere, resplend-eo, ere, *I shine, glitter* (RESPLENDENT).—5. Spoli-o, despoli-o, exspoli-o, are, *I spoil,* DESPOIL.—6. Spons-us, i; a, æ; SPOUSE,

7. spurc-us, a, um, *nasty*.
8. spu-o, ĕre, I SPIT.
9. squal-eo, ĕre, *I am dirty*.
1220. squam-a, æ, *scale* (of a fish).
1. statu-o, ĕre, *I appoint, I place*.
2. stell-a, æ, *star*.
3. steril-is, e, *barren*, STERILE.
4. stern-o, ĕre, I STREW.
5. sternu-o, ĕre, *I sneeze*.
6. stert-o, ĕre, *I snore*.
7.ᵃ stingu-o, ĕre, *I prick, erase*, (obs.)
7.ᵇ stingu-o, ĕre, *I quench*, (obs.)
8. stipul-a, æ, *straw*.
9. stirp-s, is, *stock, progeny*.
1230. st-o, are, I STAND.
1. strenu-us, a, um, *busy, diligent*, STRENUOUS.

betrothed. Sponsio, nis, *promise, pledge, bail.* Spons-or, oris, *promiser.* Sponsali-a, um, SPOUSALS, *betrothal.* Despondeo, *I betroth, give up*, DESPOND. Respondeo, *I answer*, RESPOND. Sponte, *voluntarily* (SPONTANEOUS). —7. Spum-a, æ, *foam.* Respuo, *I reject.* Con, de, ex,-spuo. —8. Squalid-us, a, um, *dirty*, SQUALID.
1221. Statu-a, æ, STATUE. Statut-um, i, STATUTE. Constituo, *I establish*, CONSTITUTE: constitutio, nis, CONSTITUTION. Destituo, *I pull down*: destitutio, nis, *deprivation*, DESTITUTION. Instituo, *I appoint*, INSTITUTE. Restituo, *I restore*: restitutio, nis, RESTITUTION. Substituo, I SUBSTITUTE.—4. Strat-um, i, *bed*, (STREET). Strag-es, is, *destruction, slaughter.* Stram-en, inis, STRAW. Constern-o, ere, *I cover*: constern-o, extern-o, are, *I alarm*, (CONSTERNATION). Prostern-o, ere, *I throw down*, PROSTRATE.—7.ᵃ Stil-us, i, *pen*, STYLE. Stimul-us, i, *goad*: stimul-o, extimul-o, instimul-o, are, *I goad*, STIMULATE. Distinguo, *I mark*, DISTINGUISH, (DISTINCT, DISTINCTION). Instingu-o, ere, instig-o, are, *I goad on*, INSTIGATE. — 7.ᵇ Exstinguo, restinguo, *I quench*, EXTINGUISH. — 8. Stipul-or, ari, I STIPULATE: adstipulor, *I assent.*—9. Exstirp-o, are, I EXTIRPATE.
1230. Stat-us, us, *standing*, STATE. Statio, nis, *standing*, STATION. Statur-a, æ, STATURE. Statim, *immediately.* Stabul-um, i, STALL, STABLE. Stam-en, inis, *thread, wool.* Stabil-is, e, *firm*, STABLE: stabil-io, constabil-io, ire, I STABLISH, ESTABLISH; instabil-is, e, *infirm*, UNSTABLE. Stagn-um, i, *standing water, pool*: stagn-o, are, I STAGNATE. Consto, *I stand firm, consist*: constat, *it is certain*: constan-s, tis, *consistent, firm*, CONSTANT: constanti-a, æ, *consistency, firmness*, CONSTANCY. Disto,

61

2. strep-o, ĕre, *I rattle, roar.*
3. strid-eo, ĕre, or strid-o, ĕre, *I creak.*
4. string-o, ĕre, *I tie, gather*, STRAIN (STRIN-GENT, STRICT, STRICTURE.)
5. stru-o, ĕre, *I build, rear.*
6. studi-um, i, *pursuit*, STUDY, *zeal.*
7. stult-us, a, um, *foolish.*
8. stup-eo, ēre, *I am amazed.*
9. suad-eo, ēre, *I persuade.*
1240. suav-is. e, SWEET.
1. sub, *under.*
2. sublim-is, e, *lofty*, SUBLIME.
3. subtil-is, e, SUBTLE, *fine-spun, refined* (subtexo).
4. sud-o, are, *I perspire.*
5. suesc-o, ĕre, *I am wont.*

I stand aloof, I am DISTANT; distanti-a, æ, DISTANCE. Exsto, *I stand out, I am* EXTANT. Insto, *I stand over, press on*, (INSTANT). Obsto, *I oppose*, (OBSTACLE): obstinat-us, a, um, OBSTINATE. Præsto, *I perform, assure, exhibit, excel*: præstanti-a, æ, *excellence*: præstò, *at hand*. Resto, *I remain*, REST. Supersto, *I stand over*, superst-es, itis, *surviving*: superstitio, nis, SUPERSTITION. Destin-o, are, *I fasten*, DESTINE: destinatio, nis, DESTINATION, (DESTINY). Ad, ante, circum, per, pro, sub,-sto, (CIRCUMSTANCE, SUBSTANCE).—2. Strepit-us, us, *noise*. Obstrepo, *I bellow against*, (OBSTREPEROUS).—3. Stridul-us. a, um, *creaking*. Strid-or, oris, *a creaking.*—4. De, di,-stringo, *I draw*, (DISTRICT). Perstringo, *I graze, thrill, dazzle*. Præstringo, *I tie up, dazzle*. Restringo, *I tie behind*, RESTRICT, RESTRAIN. Ad, con, ob, sub,-stringo, (CONSTRAIN, CONSTRAINT).—5. Stru-es, is, *heap*. Structur-a, æ, STRUCTURE. Construo, I CONSTRUCT. (CONSTRUE). Destruo, I DESTROY. Exstruo, *I build up*. Instruo, *I furnish, arrange*, INSTRUCT: instrument-um, i, INSTRUMENT. Obstruo, I OB-STRUCT. Substruo, *I build under.*—6. Studios-us, a, um, *fond, zealous*, STUDIOUS. Stud-eo, ere, *I desire, study*, (STUDENT).—7. Stultiti-a, æ, *folly.*—8. Stup-or, oris, *amazement*, STUPOUR. Stupid-us, a, um, *amazed*, STUPID.—9. Persuadeo, I PERSUADE: persuasio, suasio, nis, PERSUASION. Dissuadeo, I DISSUADE.

1240. Suavit-as, atis, *sweetness*, SUAVITY. Suavi-um, i, *kiss*: suavi-or, ari, *I kiss.*—1. Subter, *under*. Subinde, *next, now and then.*—4. Sud-or, oris, SWEAT, *labour*. De, ex,-sudo.—5. Ad, con, in,-suesco. Consuetud-o, inis, *custom*: consuefac-io, ere, *I accustom*. Desuet-us, insuet-us, a,

F

6. sug-o, ĕre, I SUCK.
7. sui, *of himself, herself, or themselves.*
8. sulc-us, i, *furrow.*
9. sum, esse, I AM.
1250. sum-o, ĕre, *I take* (sub-emo).
  1. su-o, ĕre, I SEW.
  2. super, *above.*
  3. superb-us, a, um, *proud,* SUPERB.
  4. supin-us, a, um, *lying on the back,* SUPINE.
  5. surd-us, a, um, *deaf.*
  6. su-s, is, SWINE, SOW.
  7. susurr-us, i, *whisper.*
  8. Tabern-a, æ, *tent, shop,* TAVERN.
  9. tab-es, is, *corruption, disease.*
1260. tabul-a, æ, *board,* TABLE, TABLET.
  1. tac-eo, ĕre, *I am silent.*

um, *unaccustomed.*—6. Succ-us, i, *juice.*—7. Su-us, a, um, *his, her, their own* (SUICIDE).—9. Absum, I AM ABSENT: absen-s, tis, *absent*: absenti-a, æ, ABSENCE. Adsum, *I am present.* Desum, *I am wanting.* Insum, *I am in.* Intersum, *I am at*: interest, *it concerns* (INTEREST). Obsum, *I am in the way, I injure.* Præsum, *I am over, I preside at*: præsen-s, tis, PRESENT; præsenti-a, æ, PRESENCE: repræsent-o, are, *I renew,* REPRESENT. Prosum, *I profit.* Subsum, *I am under.* Supersum, *I survive.*

1250. Sumt-us, us, *expense*: sumtuos-us, a, um, *expensive,* SUMPTUOUS. Absumo, consumo, I CONSUME: consumtio, nis, CONSUMPTION. Assumo, *I take in addition,* ASSUME. Præsumo, *I take or taste beforehand,* PRESUME. Resumo, *I take back,* RESUME.—1. Sut-or, oris, *cobbler.* As, dis, in,-suo.—2. Super-us, a, um, *upper, above*: superi-or, us, *higher,* SUPERIOR: suprem-us, summ-us, a, um, *highest, chief,* SUPREME: summ-a, æ, SUM, *headship*: consumm-o, are, *I complete,* CONSUMMATE (SUMMARY): supra, *above*: super-o, exsuper-o, are, *I exceed, surpass, overcome*: insuperabil-is, e, INSUPERABLE: sursum, *upwards.*—3. Superbi-a, æ, *pride.*—5. Absurd-us, a, um, *out of tune,* ABSURD. Obsurdesc-o, ere, *I am deaf.*—7. Susurr-o, are, *I whisper.*—8. Tabernacul-um, i, *tent,* TABERNACLE. Contuberni-um, i, *common tent* (of soldiers): contubernal-is, is, *messmate.*

1260. Tabulat-um, i, *story* (of a house). Tabell-a, æ, *tablet, ballot.*—1. Tacit-us, a, um, *silent,* TACIT: taciturn-us, a, um, *silent,* TACITURN: taciturnit-as, atis, *silence,* TACITURNITY. Conticesc-o, ere, obticeo, *I am silent*:

2. tæd-et, ēre, *it irks, tires.*
3. tal-is, e, *such.*
4. tamen, *nevertheless, yet.*
5. tang-o, ĕre, I TOUCH.
6. tant-us, a, um, *so great.*
7. tard-us, a, um, *slow,* TARDY.
8. taur-us, i, *bull.*
9. teg-o, ĕre, *I cover.*
1270. tell-us, ūris, *earth, land.*
1. tel-um, i, *dart.*
2. temerè, *inconsiderately.*
3. temet-um, i, *new wine.*
4. temn-o, ĕre, *I despise.*
5. templ-um, i, TEMPLE.
6. temp-us, oris, TIME, (TEMPORAL, TEMPORARY).
7. tend-o, ĕre, *I stretch, direct,* TEND.

reticeo, *I conceal.*—2. Tædi-um, i, *weariness, disgust,* (TEDIOUS).—4. Attamen, verumtamen, *but yet.*—5. Tact-us, us, tactio, nis, *touch* (TACT). Contamin-o, are, *I pollute,* CONTAMINATE. Attingo, contingo, *I touch, handle :* contingit, *it happens, befalls* (CONTINGENT, CONTINGENCY): contact-us, us, CONTACT : contagio, nis, CONTAGION. Obtingo, *I befall.*—6. Tantum, *so much, only.* Tantisper, *so long.* Tantopere, *so greatly.* Tam, *so.* Tamquam, *as though, as if.*--7. Tard-o, retard-o, are, *I delay,* RETARD.—9. Tegm-en, inis, *covering, roof.* Tegul-a, æ, TILE. Tign-um, i, *beam, joist.* Tog-a, æ, *gown.* Tuguri-um, i, *hut.* Teet-um, i, *roof, dwelling.* Detego, *I uncover,* DETECT. Protego, I PROTECT. Retego, I *uncover, open.* Con, in, ob,-tego: integument-um, i, INTEGUMENT.

1272. Temerit-as, atis, *rashness,* TEMERITY. Temerari-us, a, um, *rash.* Temer-o, are, *I violate.*—3. Temulent-us, a, um, *inebriated.* Abstemi-us, a, um, ABSTEMIOUS.—4. Contemno, *I despise,* CONTEMN : contemt-us, us, CONTEMPT : contumeli-a, æ, *insult,* CONTUMELY : contumelios-us, a, um, *insulting,* CONTUMELIOUS.—5. Contempl-or, ari, *I view,* CONTEMPLATE.—6. Tempest-as, atis, *season, weather,* TEMPEST : tempestiv-us, a, um, *seasonable, early.* Temper-o, are, *I mix,* TEMPER, *govern, refrain :* temperatio, nis, temperament-um, i, *government,* (TEMPERAMENT): temperan-s, tis, temperat-us, a, um, *self-restrained,* TEMPERATE : temperanti-a, æ, *self-restraint,* TEMPERANCE. Temperi-es, ei, *weather,* TEMPER : obtemper-o, are, *I obey.*—7. Tentori-um, i, TENT. Attendo, I ATTEND : attentio,

64

8. tenebr-æ, arum, *darkness*, (teneo).
9. ten-eo, ēre, *I hold*, (TENANT, TENURE, TENABLE).
1280. tener, a, um, TENDER.
    1. tenu-is, e, *slight*.
    2. tep-eo, ēre, *I am warm*.
    3. ter-es, ĕtis, *rounded*.
    4.ᵃ terg-o, ĕre,   } *I wipe*, (TERSE).
    4.ᵇ terg-eo, ēre, }
    5. terg-um, i, *a back*.
    6. termin-us, i, *boundary, end*, TERM.
    7. ter-o, ĕre, *I rub*.

nis, ATTENTION. Contendo, *I stretch*, CONTEND: conteutio, nis, CONTENTION, *exertion*. Distendo, *I stretch asunder*, DISTEND. Extendo, I EXTEND. Intendo, *I stretch, direct, increase*, INTEND: intentio, nis, *increase*, INTENTION: intent-o, are, *I brandish, hold against*. Ostend-o, ere, ostent-o, are, *I shew*, (OSTEN-SIBLE): ostentatio, nis, *showing*, OSTENTATION. Portendo, I PORTEND: portent-um, i, PORTENT: portentos-us, a, um, PORTENTOUS. Prætendo, *I hold forth*, PRETEND. De, ob, pro, re,-tendo.—9. Ten-ax, acis, *holding fast*, TENACIOUS: pertin-ax, acis, *holding fast, persisting*, PERTINACIOUS: pertinaci-a, æ, PER-TINACITY. Ten-or, oris, TENOUR. Tent-o, are, *I try*, TEMPT: tentatio, nis, *trial*, TEMPTATION: attento, I ATTEMPT: per, præ,-tento. Abstineo, I ABSTAIN: abstinenti-a, æ, ABSTINENCE, *self-restraint*. Attineo, *I belong*, ATTAIN. Contineo, *I hold*, CONTAIN. Continen-s, tis, CONTINENT: continenti-a, æ, *self-restraint*, CONTINENCE: continu-us, a, um, CONTINUOUS: continu-o, are, I CONTINUE: content-us, a, um, CONTENT. Detineo, I DETAIN. Obtineo, I OBTAIN, *hold*. Pertineo, I PERTAIN, (IMPERTINENT, APPERTAIN). Retineo, *I hold back*, RETAIN. Sustin-eo, ere, sustent-o, are, I SUSTAIN, (SUSTENANCE).
1281. Tenu-o, attenu-o, extenu-o, are, *I lessen*, ATTENUATE, EXTENUATE.—2. Tep-or, oris, *warmth*. Tepid-us, a, um, TEPID.—4. Abs, de, ex,-tergo, or tergeo.—5. Terg-us, oris, *hide*. Tergivers-or, ari, *I turn my back*, (TERGIVERSATION).—6. Termin-o, are, *I bound*, TERMINATE: determino, *I mark out*, DETERMINE: extermino, *I banish*, EXTERMINATE.—7. Terebr-o, are, *I bore*. Trit-us, a, um, *worn*, TRITE. Attero, contero, *I wear away*, (CONTRITE, CONTRITION). Detero, *I rub off*: detriment-um, i, *rubbing off*, DETRIMENT. Protero, *I tread down*: proterv-us, a, um, *wanton, bold*.—

8. terr-a, æ, *earth, land.*
9. terr-eo, ēre, *I frighten.*
1290. test-is, is, *witness,* (TEST).
1. tet-er, ra, rum, *foul.*
2. tex-o, ĕre, *I weave.*
3. theatr-um, i, THEATRE.
4. tibi-a, æ, *shin, flute.*
5. tigr-is, idis or is, TIGER.
6. tim-eo, ēre, *I fear.*
7. ting-o, ĕre, *I dip, stain,* TINGE.
8. tir-o, nis, *recruit.*
9. titul-us, i, TITLE, *inscription.*
1300. toler-o, are, *I endure,* TOLERATE.
1. toll-o, ĕre, *I raise, take away.*
2. tond-eo, ēre, *I shear, shave.*
3. ton-o, are, *I thunder.*
4. torp-eo, ēre, *I am heavy, dull.*
5. torqu-eo, ēre, *I twist* (TORTUOUS, TORTURE).

8. Terren-us, a, um, terrestr-is, e, *on land, earthly,* TERRESTRIAL. Territori-um, i, TERRITORY. Subterrane-us, a, um, SUBTERRANEOUS.—9. Terr-or, oris, TERROUR. Terribil-is, e, TERRIBLE. Terrific-o, are, I TERRIFY. Deterreo, I DETER. Abs, con, ex, per,-terreo.

1290. Testimoni-um, i, TESTIMONY. Testific-or, ari, *I bear witness,* TESTIFY. Test-or, attest-or, ari, *I witness,* ATTEST: testament-um, i, *will,* TESTAMENT: intestat-us, a, um, *without will,* INTESTATE: contestor, *I call evidence, establish,* CONTEST: detestor, *I curse,* DETEST: obtestor, I PROTEST *against:* antestor, *I summon as evidence.*—2. Text-um, i, textur-a, æ, tel-a, æ, *web,* TEXTURE, (TEXT). Contexo, *I weave together;* context-us, us, CONTEXT. Prætexo, *I border, cover;* prætext-us, us, PRETEXT: prætext-a, æ, (toga) *the gown of office at Rome.* At, de, in, inter, per, re, sub,-texo. Subtem-en, inis, *warp, web.*—4. Tibic-en, inis, *flute-player.* —6. Tim-or, oris, *fear,* (TIMOROUS). Timid-us, a, um, TIMID. Ex, per,-timesco.

1300. Toleranti-a, æ, *endurance,* TOLERANCE. Tolerabil-is, e, TOLERABLE.—1. Extollo, *I raise up,* EXTOL. At, sus,-tollo.—2. Tons-or, oris, *barber.* Intons-us, a, um, *unshaven, unshorn.* At, de,-tondeo.—3. Tonitru, u, tonitru-um, i, *thunder.* Attonit-us, a, um, ASTONISHED. De, in,-tono, (INTONATION).—4. Torp-or, oris, TORPOUR. Torpid-us, a, um, TORPID.—5. Torqu-is, is, *chain.* Tort-or, oris, *torturer.* Torment-um, i, TORMENT. Distorqueo, I

F3

6. torr-eo, ēre, *I roast.*
7. torv-us, a, um, *grim.*
8. tor-us, i, *couch, muscle.*
9. tot, *so many.*
1310. tot-us, a, um, *whole,* TOTAL.
1. trab-s, is, *beam, stripe.*
2. trah-o, ēre, I DRAW.
3. tranquill-us, a, um, TRANQUIL.
4. trans, *across.*
5. trem-o, ēre, I TREMBLE.
6. trepid-us, a, um, *trembling* (tremo).
7. tres, tria, THREE.
8. trib-us, ūs, TRIBE.
9. tric-æ, arum, *embarrassments* (TRICK).
1320. trist-is, e, *sad.*
1. tritic-um, i, *wheat.*
2. triumph-us, i, TRIUMPH.
3. trud-o, ēre, I THRUST.

DISTORT. Extorqueo, I EXTORT. Retorqueo, *I twist back,* RETORT. Con, de, in, ob,-torqueo (CONTORTION). Tortil-is, e, *twisted.*—6. Torr-is, is, *brand.* Torren-s, tis, TORRENT. Torrid-us, a, um, *scorching,* TORRID. Test-a, æ, *jar* (of earthenware). Testud-o, inis, *tortoise.*
1012. Tract-us, us, *drawing,* TRACT, TRAIT. Tract-o, are, *I handle,* TREAT : tractabil-is, e, TRACTABLE : detrecto, *I avoid,* DETRACT : obtrecto, *I disparage :* retracto, *I handle again,* RETRACT ; at, con, per,-trecto. Abstraho, *I draw off,* ABSTRACT. Attraho, *I draw to,* ATTRACT. Contraho, *I draw together,* CONTRACT. Detraho, *I draw from,* DETRACT. Distraho, *I draw asunder,* DISTRACT. Extraho, *I draw out,* EXTRACT. Protraho, *I draw forth,* PROTRACT. Retraho, *I draw back,* RETRACT. Subtraho, *I draw away,* SUBTRACT.—5. Trem-or, oris, *trembling,* TREMOUR. Tremend-us, a, um, TREMENDOUS. Tremul-us, a, um, TREMULOUS. Tremefacio, *I cause to tremble.* Tremisc-o, contrem-o, contremisc-o, ere, *I tremble.*—6. Trepid-o, are, *I tremble ;* trepidatio, nis, TREPIDATION. Intrepid-us, a, um, INTREPID.—7. Tríp-us, odis, TRIPOD. Tripl-ex, icis, *threefold,* TRIPLE. Triangul-um, i, TRIANGLE, &c.—8. Tribun-us, i, TRIBUNE. Tribunal, is, TRIBUNAL. Tribu-o, ere, *I afford, assign :* tribut-um, i, TRIBUTE : retribuo, *I give back* (RETRIBUTION): at, con, dis,-tribuo, I AT, CON, DIS,-TRIBUTE.—9. Extric-o, are, I EXTRICATE.
1320. Tristiti-a, æ, *sadness.* — 3. Abstrudo, *I hide away* (ABSTRUSE). Intrudo, I INTRUDE. Obtrudo, I

4. trunc-us, a, um, *lopped, headless.*
5. tru-x, cis, (Adj.) *savage.*
6. tu, tui, THOU.
7. tu-us, a, um, THY, THINE (tu).
8. tub-a, æ, *trumpet.*
9. tu-eor, ĕri, *I observe.*
1330. tum, *then.*
1. tum-eo, ēre, *I swell.*
2. tumul-us, i, *mound,* TOMB (tumeo).
3. tumult-us, us, *uproar,* TUMULT (tumeo).
4. tunc, *then.*
5. tund-o, ĕre, *I hammer.*
6. tunic-a, æ, TUNIC.
7. turb-a, æ, *crowd,* TROUBLE.
8. turp-is, e, *ugly, base.*
9. turr-is, is, TOWER.
1340. tu-s, ris, *frankincense.*
1. tuss-is, is, *cough.*
2. tut-us, a, um, *safe* (tueor).
3.ᵃ Uber, is, (Adj.) *fruitful.*
3.ᵇ uber, is, *teat, fertility.*
4. ubi, *where, when.*
5. ud-us (or uvid-us), a, um, *moist.*
6. ulcisc-or, i, *I avenge.*

OBTRUDE. Protrudo, I PROTRUDE. Con, de, ex,-trudo.—
4. Trunc-us, i, TRUNK. Trunc-o, de, ob,-trunc-o, are,
I lop off.—5. Trucid-o, are, *I massacre.*—8. Tubic-en, inis,
trumpeter.—9. Tuitio, nis, TUITION. Tut-or, oris,
guardian, TUTOR. Tutel-a, æ, *guardianship,* TUTELAGE.
Intu-eor, eri, *I look at, observe* (INTUITION). Obtueor,
I gaze at; obtut-us, us, *gaze.*
1331. Tumid-us, a, um, *swelling, swoln,* TUMID. Tum-or, oris,
swelling, TUMOUR. Contum-ax, acis, CONTUMACIOUS.
Tumul-o, contumul-o, are, *I entomb.*—3. Tumultuos-us, a,
um, TUMULTUOUS. Tumultu-or, ari, *I make an
uproar.*—5. Obtund-o, *I deafen, blunt* (OBTUSE). Retundo,
I blunt. Contundo, *I hammer, beat, defeat* (CONTUSION).
Extundo, *I hammer out.*—7. Turbid-us, a, um, TURBID.
Turbulent-us, a, um, TURBULENT. Turb-o, inis,
whirlwind. Turb-o, con, de, dis, ex, ob, per, pro,-turb-o,
are, I DISTURB, PERTURB (DISTURBANCE, PER-
TURBATION).—8. Turpitud-o, inis, *baseness, ugliness,*
TURPITUDE.
1343.ᵃ Ubert-as, atis, *fruitfulness..*—4. Ubique, *everywhere.*
Ubicunque, *whensoever, wheresoever.* — 5. Sud-us, a,

68

7. ull-us, a, um, *any* (unus).
8. ulm-us, i, ELM-*tree*.
9. uln-a, æ, *arm*, ELL.
1350. ulter, a, um, *farther* (obs.).
1. umbr-a, æ, *shade* (UMBRAGE, UMBRELLA).
2. unci-a, æ, OUNCE, INCH.
3. unc-us, a, um, *hooked*.
4. und-a, æ, *wave* (UNDULATE).
5. unde, *whence*.
6. ung-o, ĕre, I ANOINT.
7. ungu-is, is, *nail, talon*.
8. unquam, *at any time*.
9. un-us, a, um, ONE, (UNIT, UNITY, UNISON).
1360. urb-s, is, *city*.
1. urg-eo, ĕre, *I press*, URGE, (URGENT).
2. urn-a, æ, *pitcher*, URN.
3. ur-o, ĕre, *I burn*.
4.ₐ urs-us, i, *bear*.
4.ᵦ urs-a, æ, *she-bear*.
5. usque, *even to, even*.
6. ut, uti, *that, as, &c.*
7. ut-er, ra, rum, *which of two*, EITHER.
8. ut-or, i, I USE.

um, *dry.*—6. Ult-or, oris, *avenger.* Ultio, nis, *vengeance.*
Inult-us, a, um, *unavenged, unpunished.*—7. Null-us, a,
um, *none;* nonnull-us, a, um, *some.*
1350. Ultro, *beyond, voluntarily.* Ultra, *beyond:* ulteri-or, us,
further; ultim-us, a, um, *furthest, last.*—1. Umbr-o, ad, in,
ob,-umbr-o, are, *I shade.*—4. Und-o, are, *I fluctuate:*
abundo, I ABOUND: inundo, I INUNDATE : redundo,
I overflow, flow back, REDOUND.—5. Undique, *on all
sides.*—6. Unguent-um, i, OINTMENT. Unctio, nis,
UNCTION.—7. Ungul-a, æ, *hoof.*—8. Nunquam, *never.*—
9. Unà, *together.* Unusquisque, unaquæque, unumquod-
que, *each one.* Unic-us, a, um, ONLY, UNIQUE.
Unanim-is, e, UNANIMOUS. Univers-us, a, um, *all,*
UNIVERSAL: univers-um, i, UNIVERSE.
1360. Urban-us, a, um, *of the city,* URBAN, *polite,* URBANE.
Suburbi-um, i, SUBURB. — 3. Comburo, *I burn up,*
(COMBUSTION). Inuro, *I brand,* INURE. Ad, amb,
de, ex, per, præ,-uro.—5. Usquam, *anywhere;* nusquam,
nowhere. — 6. Utinam, O *that.* — 7. Uterque, utraque,
utrumque, *each (of two).* Utrum, *whether.* Neut-er, ra,
rum, NEITHER.—8. Util-is, e, USEFUL : utilit-as, atis,
UTILITY. Us-us, us, *custom,* USE, (USUAL): usurp-o,

9. uv-a, æ, *grape.*

1370. ux-or, ōris, *wife,* (ungo).

1. Vacc-a, æ, *cow,* (VACCINATE).
2. vac-o, are, *I am at leisure, free, empty* (VACANT).
3. vad-o, ĕre, *I go.*
4. vaf-er, ra, rum, *crafty.*
5. vag-us, a, um, *wandering,* VAGUE.
6. val-eo, ēre, *I am strong, well, able,* I AVAIL.
7. vall-is, is, VALLEY, VALE.
8. vall-us, i, *rampart,* WALL.
9. van-us, a, um, *empty,* VAIN.

1380. vap-or, ōris, VAPOUR.

1. vari-us, a, um, VARIOUS.
2.ᵃ vas, vasis, VESSEL.
2.ᵇ vas, vadis, *surety.*
3. vast-us, a, um, VAST, WASTE.
4. vat-es, is, *seer, poet.*
5. vehemen-s, tis, (Adj.) *forcible, earnest,* VEHE-
6. veh-o, ĕre, *I carry.* [MENT.

---

are, *I use, take, enjoy,* USURP. Usur-a, æ, USURY. Usitat-us, a, um, *accustomed.* Utensili-a, um, UTENSILS. Abutor, I ABUSE.

1372. Vacu-us, a, um, *empty, at leisure,* (EVACUATE).— 3. Vad-um, i, *a shallow,* (WADE). Evado, *I escape,* EVADE, (EVASIVE). Invado, I INVADE. Pervado, *I go over,* PERVADE. — 5. Vag-or, ari, *I wander:* vagabund-us, a, um, *wandering,* VAGABOND, VAGRANT. E, per,-vagor, (EXTRAVAGANT).—6. Convalesc-o, revalesc-o, ere, *I get well,* CONVALESCENT. Valetud-o, inis, *health, strength.* Valid-us, a, um, *strong,* VALID: invalid-us, a, um, *weak,* INVALID. Valdè, *very,* (VALUE, VALOUR, VALIANT). Prævaleo, I PREVAIL: prævalen-s, tis, PREVALENT.—8. Vall-o, are, *I entrench.* Circum, ob, præ,-vallo. — 9. Vanit-as, atis, *emptiness,* VANITY. Vanesc-o, evanesc-o, ere, I VANISH.

1881. Variet-as, atis, VARIETY. Vari-o, are, I VARY.— 2.ᵇ Vadimoni-um, i, *bail.*—3. Vast-o, devast-o, are, *I waste,* DEVASTATE. — 4. Vaticin-or, ari, *I prophesy.* — 6. Vehicul-um, i, VEHICLE. Vex-o, are, *I harass,* VEX: vexatio, nis, *harassing,* VEXATION. Vexill-um, i, *standard, flag.* Vectigal, is, *tax, toll, tribute.* Vect-is, is, *lever.* Vi-a, æ, *way;* viat-or, oris, *traveller:* avi-us, devi-us, a, um, *out of the way,* DEVIOUS, (DEVIATE): obvi-us, a, um, *meeting,* OBVIOUS: obviam, *in the way of,* (OBVIATE): pervi-us, a, um, *accessible,* PERVIOUS: prævi-us, a, um, *going before,* PREVIOUS: invi-us, a, um,

7. vell-o, ĕre, *I pluck*.
8. vel-ox, ocis, *swift* (volo).
9. vel-um, i, VEIL, *sail* (veho).
1390. ven-a, æ, VEIN.
  1. venen-um, i, *poison*, VENOM.
  2. vener-or, ari, *I worship*, VENERATE.
  3. veni-a, æ, *pardon* (VENIAL).
  4. ven-io, ire, *I come*.
  5. ven-or, ari, *I hunt*.
  6. vent-er, ris, *belly*.
  7. vent-us, i, WIND.
  8. ven-um, *for sale* (Def.).
  9. venust-us, a, um, *lovely* (Venus).
1400. vēr, is, *spring*.
  1. verber, is, *stripe, blow*.
  2. verb-um, i, *word* (VERB, VERBAL).
  3. ver-eor, eri, *I fear*.
  4. verg-o, ĕre, *I lean*, VERGE.
  5. verm-is, is, WORM.

inaccessible : trivi-um, *a place where three roads meet, high-road :* trivial-is, e, TRIVIAL. Inveho, *I carry into,* INVEIGH, (INVECTIVE). Conveho, I CONVEY, (CONVOY): convex-us, a, um, CONVEX. A, ad, circum, de, e, per, præ, præter, pro, re, sub, trans,-veho.—7. Vell-us, eris, *fleece.* A, con, di, e, per, re, - vello, (CONVULSE, REVULSION, &c.)—8. Velocit-as, atis, *swiftness,* VELOCITY.—9. Vel-o, are, *I veil :* revelo, I UNVEIL, REVEAL, (REVELATION). Velific-o, are; or, ari, *I sail.*

1394. Advenio, *I come to :* adven-a, æ, *new-comer, stranger :* advent-us, us, *coming,* ADVENT. Circumvenio, *I surround,* CIRCUMVENT. Convenio, *I meet :* convent-us, us, *meeting,* CONVENTION (CONVENT): convenit, *it suits :* convenien-s, tis, *suitable,* CONVENIENT. Evenit, *it happens ;* event-us, us, EVENT. Invenio, *I find,* INVENT. Intervenio, I INTERVENE : obvenio, *I meet, befall.* Prævenio, *I come before,* PREVENT. De, per, pro, sub, super,-venio.—5. Venat-or, oris, *huntsman.* Venabul-um, i, *hunting-spear.*—7. Ventil-o, are, *I fan,* VENTILATE.—8. Venal-is, e, *on sale,* VENAL. Vend-o, ere, *I sell,* VEND. Ven-eo, ire, *I am sold.*—9. Venust-as, atis, *beauty, elegance.*

1400. Vern-us, a, um, VERNAL.—1. Verber-o, are, *I beat.* De, di, trans,-verbero.—2. Proverbi-um, i, PROVERB. Adverbi-um, i, ADVERB.—3. Verecund-us, a, um, *bashful, modest :* verecundi-a, æ, *modesty, timidity.* Revereor, I REVERE : reverenti-a, æ, REVERENCE.—4. Convergo, I CONVERGE.

6. vern-a, æ, *born-slave*.
7. verr-o, ĕre, *I sweep*.
8. vert-o, ĕre, *I turn*.
9. ver-us, a, um, *true*, VERY.
†10. vesc-or, i, *I eat*.
1. vesp-a, æ, WASP.
2. vesper, i, and is, *evening*.
3. vestigi-um, i, *footstep*, VESTIGE.
4. vest-is, is, *garment*, VEST, VESTURE.
5. vet-o, are, *I forbid*.
6. vet-us, eris, (Adj.) *ancient*.
7. vibr-o, are, *I shake*, VIBRATE.
8. vicis, *change, turn* (Def.).

Divergo, I DIVERGE.—6. Vernacul-us, a, um, VERNA-CULAR.—8. Vert-ex, icis, *top* (VERTICAL). Vort-ex, icis, *whirlpool*. Vertig-o, inis, *whirl, swoon*. Versus, *towards*: adversus, adversum, *towards, against*: rursus, rursum, *backward, again*: seorsum, *apart*. Vers-us, us, *order*, VERSE. Versut-us, a, um, *shifty, skilful*. Vers-o, are, *I turn, ply*: vers-or, ari, *I am engaged*, VERSED: versatil-is, e, VERSATILE: convers-or, ari, I CONVERSE (CONVERSATION). Averto, *I turn away*, AVERT: avers-us, a, um, *turned from*, AVERSE: avers-or, ari, *I shrink from, abhor*. Adverto, *I turn to*, ADVERT: advers-us, a, um, *opposed*, ADVERSE: advers-or, ari, *I oppose*: adversarius, i, ADVERSARY. Converto, *I turn*, CONVERT: conversio, nis, *change*, CONVERSION: controversi-a, æ, CONTROVERSY. Diverto, *I turn aside*, DIVERT: divers-us, a, um, *divided, different*: divorti-um, i, *separation*, DIVORCE. Everto, *I overthrow*. Inverto, I INVERT. Perverto, I PERVERT: pervers-us, a, um, PERVERSE. Præverto, *I anticipate*. Reverto, *I turn back*, REVERT. Subverto, I SUBVERT. Transvers-us, a, um, TRANSVERSE. Obverto, *I turn towards*: obvers-or, ari, *I am turned towards, I occur*. Ante, de,-verto.—9. Verùm, verò, *truly, but truly*. Verè, *truly*, VERY. Ver-ax, acis, *true-spoken*, VERACIOUS (VERACITY). Ver-um, i, *the truth*. Verit-as, atis, *truth*, VERITY, (VERITABLE).

1412. Vesper-a, æ, *evening*. Vespertin-us, a, um, *at evening*, VESPER. Vesperascit, advesperascit, *it grows towards evening*. Vespertilio, nis, *bat*.—3. Vestig-o, investig-o, are, *I track*, INVESTIGATE. — 4. Vest-io, convest-io, ire, *I clothe* (INVEST): vestit-us, us, *clothing*: vestiment-um, i, *garment*, VESTMENT.—6. Vetust-us, a, um, *ancient*: vetust-as, atis, *antiquity*. Veteran-us, i, VETERAN, Inveterat-us, a, um, INVETERATE: inveterasc-o, ere, *I grow old in*.—8. Vicissim, *by turns*. Vicissitud-o, inis,

9. vic-us, i, *street*.
1420. vid-eo, ēre, *I see*.
1. vig-eo, ēre, *I flourish* (vis).
2. vigil, is, (Adj.) *watchful* (vigeo).
3. vil-is, e, *cheap*, VILE.
4. vill-a, æ, *country-house*.
5. vinc-io, ire, *I bind*.
6. vinc-o, ĕre, *I conquer*.
7. vindic-o, are, *I avenge, claim*, VINDICATE.
8. vin-um, i, WINE.
9. viol-a, æ, VIOLET.
1430. vir, i, *man, husband* (vis).
1. vir-eo, ēre, *I am green* (vis).
2. virt-us, utis, VIRTUE, *valour* (vir).
3. vir-us, i, *poison* (VIRULENT).
4. vis, *strength* (Def.).
5. vit-is, is, *vine*.
6. viti-um, i, *fault*, VICE.

change, VICISSITUDE. Vicari-us, i, *substitute, successor*, VICARIOUS (VICAR).—9. Vicin-us, a, um, *neighbouring*: vicini-a, æ, vicinit-as, atis, *neighbourhood*, VICINITY.
1420. Vis-us, us, vis-um, i, visio, nis, *sight*, VISION. Vis-o, ere, visit-o, are, invis-o, ere, *I go to see*, VISIT. Eviden-s, tis, EVIDENT. Invideo, I ENVY, *grudge*: invis-us, a, um, *hated*. Provideo, *I foresee*, PROVIDE: providen-s, tis, provid-us, a, um, *foreseeing*, PROVIDENT: providenti-a, æ, *foresight*, PROVIDENCE, PROVISION. Improvis-us, a, um, *unforeseen*. Per, præ, re,-video.—1. Vig-or, oris, VIGOUR.—2. Vigili-a, æ, *watch*, VIGIL. Vigil-o, ad, e, in, per,-vigil-o, are, *I watch*: vigilan-s, tis, VIGILANT. — 4. Villic-us, i, *steward*.—5. Vincul-um, i, *chain*. De, e, re, -vincio.—6. Victim-a, æ, VICTIM. Vict-or, oris, victr-ix, icis, *conqueror*, VICTORIOUS: victori-a, æ, VICTORY. Convinco, I CONVINCE, CONVICT. Invict-us, a, um, INVINCIBLE. Pervic-ax, acis, *obstinate*. Provinci-a, æ, PROVINCE. De, per, re,-vinco.—7. Vindici-æ, arum, *claim*. Vindict-a, æ, *vengeance, protection, liberating wand* (VINDICTIVE). Vind-ex, icis, *avenger, defender*.—8. Vine-a, æ, VINE, *vineyard*. Vindemi-a, æ, *vintage*.
1430. Viril-is, e, *manly*. Virg-o, inis, VIRGIN.—1. Virid-is, e, *green*: viridan-s, tis, VERDANT: viridit-as, atis, VERDURE. Viret-um, i, *greenery, grove*. Viresco, reviresco, *I become green*. Virg-a, æ, *twig, rod*: virgult-um, i, *shrub*.—4. Violen-s, tis, violent-us, a, um, VIOLENT. Viol-o, are, I VIOLATE.—6. Vitios-us, a, um, *faulty*, VITIOUS. Vituper-o, are, *I reproach*, VITUPERATE:

7. vit-o, are, I AVOID.
8. vitul-us, i, *calf*, (VEAL, VELLUM).
9. viv-o, ĕre, *I live.*
1440. vix, *scarcely.*
  1. voc-o, are, *I call.*
  2. vol-o, velle, *I wish,* WILL, (Irreg.)
  3. vol-o, are, *I fly.*
  4. volv-o, ĕre, *I roll, turn over.*
  5. vomer, is, *ploughshare,* (vomo).
  6. vom-o, ĕre, I VOMIT.

Viti-o, are, *I taint,* VITIATE.—7. De, e,-vito.—9. Viv-us, a, um, *alive :* vivid-us, a, um, *lively,* VIVID. Viv-ax, acis, *lively, long-lived,* VIVACIOUS (VIVACITY). Vict-us, us, *manner of living, livelihood, food,* VICTUALS. Vit-a, æ, *life :* vital-is, e, VITAL. Viper-a, æ, VIPER. Convivo, *I live with :* conviv-a, æ, *guest :* convivi-um, i, *banquet* (CONVIVIAL); convict-us, us, *society :* conviv-or, ari, *I banquet.* Revivisco, I REVIVE : rediviv-us, a, um, *revived.* Supervivo, I SURVIVE.

1441. Vocatio, nis, *calling,* VOCATION. Vo-x, cis, VOICE : vocal-is, c, *speaking, tuneful,* VOCAL : vocul-a, æ, *voice,* VOWEL : vocifer-or, ari, *I cry out,* VOCIFERATE : convici-um, i, *reproach ;* convici-or, ari, *I reproach.* Vocabul-um, i, *word.* Avoco, *I call off,* (AVOCATION). Advoco, *I call to ;* advocat-us, i, ADVOCATE. Convoco, I CON-VOKE : convocatio, nis, CONVOCATION. Invoco, I INVOKE : Provoco, *I challenge, appeal,* PROVOKE. Revoco, *I call back,* REVOKE. De, e, se,-voco.—2. Volunt-as, atis, *wish, will :* voluntari-us, a, um, VOLUNTARY. Volup-is, e, *pleasant ;* volupt-as, atis, *pleasure,* (VOLUPTUOUS) : voluptari-us, a, um, *given to pleasure,* VOLUPTUARY. Vel, ve, *or, even ;* velut, *as.* Benevol-us, a, um; benevolen-s, tis, BENEVOLENT : benevolenti-a, æ, *goodwill,* BENEVOLENCE. Malevol-us, a, um, MALEVOLENT; malevolenti-a, æ, *illwill,* MALE-VOLENCE. Malo, *I had rather, I prefer.* Nolo, *I will not, I am unwilling.*—3. Volat-us, us, *flight.* Volatil-is, e, *flying,* VOLATILE. Voluc-er, ris, re, *swift ;* volucr-is, is, *bird.* Volit-o, are, *I flit, fly ;* in, per, super,-volito. A, ad, ante, circum, con, de, e, in, per, præter, pro, re, sub, super, trans,-vol-o, are.—4. Volut-o, are, *I roll, turn over.* Volubil-is, e, *rolling,* VOLUBLE. Volum-en, inis, *roll,* VOLUME. Valv-æ, arum, *folding-doors.* Devolvo, *I roll down,* DEVOLVE. Evolvo, *I unroll, roll out,* EVOLVE : evolutio, nis, *unrolling, perusal,* (EVOLUTION). Involvo, *I wrap,* INVOLVE : involucr-um, i, *wrapper.* Revolvo, *I roll back,* REVOLVE, (REVOLUTION). Ad, circum, con, ob, per, pro, sub,-volvo.—6. Con, e, re,-vomo.—

G

7. vor-o, are, *I devour.*
8. vos, *ye.*
9. vov-eo, ēre, I VOW.
1450. vulg-us, i, *common people.*
  1. vuln-us, eris, WOUND.
  2. vulp-es, is, *fox.*
  3. vultur, is, VULTURE.
  4. vult-us, us, *countenance.*
  5. Zon-a, æ, *girdle,* ZONE.

———

ADDENDA.

  6. Acer, is, *maple-tree.*
  7. acerr-a, æ, *censer.*
  8. ærumn-a, æ, *sorrow.*
  9. alg-eo, ēre, *I am cold.*
1460. aln-us, i, ALDER-*tree.*
  1. apud, *at, near, in.*
  2. arm-us, i, *shoulder,* (ARM).
  3. aut, *or.*
  4. Balte-us, i, BELT.
  5. bis, *twice.*
  6. buccin-a, æ, *trumpet.*
  7. bux-us, i, BOX-*tree.*
  8. Call-us, i, *hard skin, hardness.*
  9. cann-a, æ, CANE.
1470. cerebr-um, i, *brain.*
  1. clitell-æ, arum, *panniers.*

7· Vor-ax, acis, VORACIOUS. Vorag-o, inis, *vortex, abyss.* Devoro, I DEVOUR.—8. Vest-er, ra, rum, *your.*—9. Vot-um, i, *vow, prayer, wish,* (VOTE): votiv-us, a, um, VOTIVE. Devoveo, I DEVOTE: devotio, nis, DEVOTION.
1450. Vulgo, *commonly.* Vulgar-is, e, *common,* VULGAR. Vulg-o, e, per,-vulg-o, are, *I publish,* DIVULGE.— 1. Vulner-o, convulner-o, are, *I wound,* (INVULNERABLE). — 9. Algid-us, a, um, *cold.*
1462. Armill-a, æ, ARMLET.—8. Callos-us, a, um, CALLOUS. Call-eo, ere, *I am hardened, skilled:* hence callid-us.

2. colum-en, inis, *prop, stay*.
3. concinn-us, a, um, *neat, elegant*.
4. crem-o, are, *I burn*.
5. cune-us, i, *wedge, bench*.
6. curt-us, a, um, *short, deficient*.
7. Delphin, is, DOLPHIN.
8. delubr-um, i, *shrine, temple*.
9. Fastigi-um, i, *coping, pinnacle, summit*.
1480. favill-a, æ, *ashes*.
 1. ferè, fermè, *almost*.
 2. fil-um, i, *thread*, FILAMENT.
 3. Glom-us, eris, *ball of wool*.
 4. glut-en, inis, GLUE.
 5. Har-a, æ, *stye*.
 6. histori-a, æ, HISTORY.
 7. horre-um, i, *barn*.
 8. hosti-a, æ, *victim*.
 9. Ili-a, um, *bowels*.
1490. imbu-o, ĕre, *I steep*, IMBUE.
 1. jejun-us, a, um, *fasting, meagre*.
 2. jub-a, æ, *mane*.
 3. Lamp-as, adis, *torch*, LAMP.
 4. lani-o, are, *I tear*.
 5. lat-ex, icis, *liquor*.
 6. Manc-us, a, um, *imperfect*.
 7. mand-o, ĕre, *I eat*.
 8. merul-a, æ, *blackbird*.
 9. modi-us, i, *bushel*.
1500. myrrh-a, æ, MYRRH.
 1. Nimb-us, i, *cloud*.
 2. Pene, *almost*.
 3. pale-a, æ, *straw*.
 4. pann-us, i, *rag*.
 5. pater-a, æ, } *bowl, dish*.
    patin-a, æ, }

1472. Column-a, æ, *pillar*, COLUMN.   Incolum-is, e, *safe, unharmed*.—3. Concinn-o, are, *I arrange, make*.—5. Cune-o, are, *I wedge in*.

1483. Glomer-o, conglomer-o, are, *I wind, gather, assemble*.

1492. Jubar, is, *sun-beam*. — 4. Lani-us, i, *butcher*.   Di-lanio, *I tear asunder*.—7. Maxill-a, æ, mal-a, æ, *jaw*.

6. pav-io, ire, *I strike*, PAVE.
7. pern-ix, icis, (Adj.) *fleet*.
8. pharetr-a, æ, *quiver*.
9. phaler-æ, arum, *trappings*.
1510. pic-us, i, *woodpecker*, PYE.
   1. pil-a, æ, PILLAR, *ball*, (PILL), *mortar*.
   2. pil-us, i, *a hair, a company*.
   3. pil-um, i, *javelin*.
   4. pins-o, ĕre, *I pound*.
   5. placent-a, æ, *cake*.
   6. plang-o, ĕre, *I beat*.
   7. platan-us, i, PLANE-*tree*.
   8. plate-a, æ, *street*.
   9. plumb-um, i, *lead*.
1520. pocul-um, i, *cup*.
   1. poll-eo, ĕre, *I have power*.
   2. poll-ex, icis, *thumb*.
   3. pol-us, i, POLE, *sky*.
   4. pont-us, i, *sea*.
   5. popin-a, æ, *cook-shop*.
   6. popl-es, itis, *knee*.
   7. procer-es, um, *nobles*.
   8. pror-a, æ, PROW.
   9. pruin-a, æ, *hoar-frost*.
1530. prun-us, i, PLUM-*tree*.
   1. psall-o, ĕre, *I play and sing*, (PSALM).
   2. psittac-us, i, *parrot*.
   3. pull-us, i, *chicken*, (PULLET).
   4. pulmo, nis, *lung*, (PULMONARY).
   5. pul-s, tis, *pottage*, (PULSE).
   6. pulvin-us, i; ar, is, *cushion*.
   7. pupp-is, is, *stern*, POOP.
   8. pup-us, i; a, æ, *doll*, PUPPET.
   9. pute-us, i, *well*.
1540. putr-is, e, *rotten*, PUTRID.
   1. Rat-is, is, *bark*, RAFT.

1506. Paviment-um, i, PAVEMENT.
1514. Pist-or, oris, *baker*.   Pistill-um, i, PESTLE.—6. Planct-us, us, *beating, lamentation*.
1538. Pupill-us, i, *ward*, PUPIL.
1540. Putresc-o, ere, *I grow putrid*.   Putrefac-io, ere, *I make putrid*, (PUTREFACTION).

2. redim-io, ire, *I encircle, I crown.*
3. rest-is, is, *rope.*
4. retro, *backward,* (RETROGRADE, RETROSPECT, &c.
5. re-us, a, um, *accused, defendant,* (res).
6. rhed-a, æ, *car.*
7. rhetor, is, RHETORICIAN.
8. rim-a, æ, *chink.*
9. rog-us, i, *funeral-pyre.*
1550. rub-us, i, *raspberry-tree, bramble.*
1. Satell-es, itis, *bodyguard,* SATELLITE.
2. sauci-us, a, um, *wounded.*
3. sceptr-um, i, SCEPTRE.
4. scut-um, i, *shield.*
5. scyph-us, i, *cup.*
6. sentin-a, æ, SINK.
7. sent-is, is, *thorn.*
8. sic-a, æ, *poniard.*
9. socer, i, *father-in-law.*
1560. sodal-is, is, *comrade.*
1. sole-a, æ, *sandal,* SOLE.
2. son-s, tis, *guilty.*
3. stip-o, are, *I close in.*
4. stip-s, is, *fee, alms.*
5. stomach-us, i, STOMACH.
6. strangul-o, are, I STRANGLE.
7. Tæd-a, æ, *pine, torch.*
8. talent-um, i, TALENT.
9. talp-a, æ, *mole.*
1570. tal-us, i, *ancle, die,* (TALON).
1. tax-us, i, *yew-tree.*
2. temo, nis, *pole.*
3. tesser-a, æ, *ticket, watchword.*
4. thalam-us, i, *chamber.*
5. thym-um, i, THYME.
6. tili-a, æ, *linden-tree.*
7. tine-a, æ, *moth.*
8. tragœdi-a, æ, TRAGEDY.

1558. Sicari-us, i, *assassin.*
1560. Sodalit-as, atis; sodaliti-um, i, *society, club.* Inson-s, tis, *innocent.*—4. Stipendi-um, i, *pay,* STIPEND.
1578. Tragic-us, a, um, TRAGIC.
G3

9. transtr-um, i, *beam, deck.*
1580. trutin-a, æ, *scale.*
　1. turd-us, i, THRUSH.
　2. turg-eo, ēre, *I swell.*
　3. turtur, is, TURTLE-*dove.*
　4. tyrann-us, i, TYRANT.
　5. Ulul-o, are, I HOWL.
　6. umb-o, nis, *boss, shield.*
　7. ut-er, ris, *bladder.*
　8. Vacill-o, are, *I totter,* VACILLATE.
　9. vagin-a, æ, *scabbard.*
1590. vag-io, ire, *I cry, squall.*
　1. vapul-o, are, *I am beaten.*
　2. veg-eo, *I am lively.*
　3. viscer-a, um, *entrails.*
　4. vitr-um, i, *glass.*
　5. vitt-a, æ, *fillet.*
　6. Xyst-us, i, *a terrace walk.*

1582. Turgid-us, a, um, *swollen,* TURGID.
1591. Veget-us, a, um, *lively, vigorous.* Veget-o, are, *I quicken,* (VEGETABLE).
1594. Vitre-us, a, um, *glassy.*—5. Vittat-us, i, um, *filleted.*

SELECT PROPER NAMES.

I.—HEATHEN DEITIES.

1. Æsculapi-us, i, *god of medicine, and son of Apollo.*
2. Amphitrit-e, es, *a sea-goddess.*
3. Apoll-o, inis, } *god of music and archery, son of*
   Phœb-us, i, } *Jupiter and Latona.*
4. Astræ-a, æ, *goddess of justice.*
5. Auror-a, æ, *goddess of morning, wife of Tithonus.*
6. Bacch-us, i, } *god of wine, son of Jupiter and Semele.*
   Liber, i, }
7. Bellon-a, æ, *goddess of war.*
8. Cer-es, eris, *goddess of corn, daughter of Saturn.*
9. Cupid-o, inis, *god of love, son of Venus.*
10. Cybel-e, es, *an ancient goddess.*
1. Dian-a, æ, *goddess of archery, sister of Apollo.*
2. Dryad-es, um, *wood-nymphs.*
3. Eos, *morning.*
4. Faun-us, i, } *god of shepherds.*
   Pan, is, }
5. Flor-a, æ, *goddess of flowers.*
6. Heb-e, es, *goddess of youth, daughter of Juno.*
7. Herm-es, æ, } *Mercury, god of gain and eloquence,*
   Mercuri-us, i, } *son of Jupiter and Maia.*
8. Hymen, is, or Hymenæ-us, i, *god of marriage.*
9. Ir-is, idis, *goddess of the rainbow, and messenger of*
20. Jan-us, i, *god of the year, with two faces.*   [*heaven.*
1. Juno, nis, *queen of heaven, wife of Jupiter.*
2. Juppiter, Jovis, *king of heaven, son of Saturn,*
   (JOVIAL).
3. Laton-a, æ, *mother of Apollo and Diana.*
4. Mar-s, tis, *god of war.*
5. Minerv-a, æ, } *goddess of wisdom.*
   Pall-as, adis, }   [*Muses.*
6. Mnemosyn-e, es, *goddess of memory, mother of the*
7. Mom-us, i, *god of jest.*
8. Morphe-us, i, *god of dreams.*
9. Mus-æ, arum, *the nine Muses.*

30. Naiad-es, or Naid-es, um, *fountain-nymphs*.
 1. Nemes-is, is, *goddess of punishment*.
 2. Neptun-us, i, *king of ocean, son of Saturn*.
 3. Nere-us, i, or os, *a sea-god*.
 4. Ocean-us, i, OCEAN.
 5. Pal-es, is, *goddess of shepherds*.
 6. Penat-es, ium, } *household gods*.
    Lar-es, ium,
 7. Pluto, nis, } *king of the shades below*.
    Dis, Ditis,
 8. Plut-us, i, *god of riches*.
 9. Pomon-a, æ, *goddess of fruits*.
40. Priap-us, i, *a deity of gardens*.
 1. Proserpin-a, æ, } *daughter of Ceres, wife of Pluto*.
    Persephon-e, es,
 2. Prote-us, i, or os, *a sea-god*.
 3. Saturn-us, i, *father of Jupiter*.   [*goat*.
 4. Satyr-i, orum, *Satyrs, rural deities, half man, half*
 5. Silvan-us, i, *god of woods*.
 6. Tethy-s, os, *goddess of the sea*.
 7. Them-is, idis, *goddess of justice*.
 8. Triton, is, *a sea-god*.
 9. Ven-us, eris, *goddess of beauty*.
50. Vertumn-us, i, *an Italian deity of gardens*.
 1. Vest-a, æ, *goddess of the hearth-fire*.
 2. Vulcan-us, i, *god of fire*.

II.—NAMES IN MYTHOLOGY.

 3. Acbill-es, is, or ei, *a Grecian chief at Troy, son of Peleus and Thetis*.
 4. Actæ-on, onis, *a hunter, changed into a stag*.
 5. Adon-is, idis, *a youth loved by Venus*.
 6. Adrast-us, i, *a king of Argos who fought against Thebes*.
 7. Æac-us, i, *a king of Ægina, made a judge in Hades*.
 8. Ægisth-us, i, *son of Thyest-es, æ*.
 9. Æet-es, æ, *king of Colchis, father of Medea*.
60. Æne-as, æ, *a Trojan hero, son of Venus & Anchis-es, æ*.
 1. Æol-us, i, *king of the winds*.
 2. Agamemn-on, onis, *son of Atre-us, i, or os, king of Mycenæ, leader of the Greeks at Troy*.
 3. Agav-e, es, *daughter of Cadmus*.

4. Aj-ax, acis, *son of Telamon, is, a Grecian chief at Troy.*
5. Aj-ax, acis, *son of Oile-us, i, or os, a Grecian chief at Troy.*
6: Alcino-us, i, *king of Phæacia.*
7. Amphi-on, onis, *a musician, builder of Thebes.*
8. Andromach-e, es, *wife of Hector.*
9. Andromed-a, æ, *a maiden saved from a sea-monster by Perseus.*
70. Antenor, is, *a Trojan prince.*
1. Antiloch-us, i, *son of Nestor.*
2. Arethus-a, æ, *a nymph changed into a fountain.*
3. Arg-o, us, *the first ship.*
4. Arg-us, i, *a hundred-eyed guardian changed into a*
5. Ariadn-e, es, *daughter of Minos.* [*peacock.*
6. Ari-on, onis, *a musician.*
7. Ascani-us, i, } *son of Æneas.*
   Jul-us, i,
8. Astyan-ax, actis, *son of Hector.*
9. Bellerophon, tis, *a Corinthian hero.*
80. Briare-us, i, *a giant, having a hundred hands.*
1. Cadm-us, i, *a Phænician, son of Agen-or, is, founder of Thebes.*
2. Calch-as, antis, *soothsayer of the Greeks at Troy.*
3. Calyps-o, us, *a nymph.*
4. Cassandr-a, æ, *daughter of Priam, a prophetess.*
5. Castor, is, *son of Led-a, æ, twin with Poll-ux, ucis.*
6. Cecrop-s, is, *founder of Athens.*
7. Centaur-i, orum, *Centaurs, half man, half horse.*
8. Cerber-us, i, *watch-dog of Hades.*
9. Chaos, *the confused mass of matter, existing before the formation of the world.*
90. Charon, tis, *ferryman of the Styx.*
1. Charybd-is, is, *a Sicilian whirlpool.*
2. Chimær-a, æ, *a fabulous monster.*
3. Chiron, is, *a Centaur, tutor of Achilles.*
4. Circ-e, es, *an enchantress, daughter of Sol.*
5. Clytemnæstr-a, æ, *daughter of Tyndarus, wife of Agamemnon.*
6. Creon, tis, (1) *king of Corinth,* (2) *king of Thebes.*
7. Cyclop-es, um, *one-eyed giants in Sicily.*
8. Dædal-us, i, *an Athenian artist and inventer.*
9. Dana-e, es, *daughter of Acrisi-us, i, and mother of Perseus, by Jupiter.*

100. Dana-us, i, *son of Belus, and father of* 50 *daughters.*
  1. Daphn-e, es, *a maiden changed into a bay-tree.*
  2. Dardan-us, i, *king of Troy.*
  3. Deucalion, is, *king of Phthia, son of Prometheus, husband of Pyrrh-a, æ.*
  4. Did-o, us, *foundress of Carthage.*   [*Troy.*
  5. Diomed-es, is, *son of Tyde-us, i, a Grecian chief at*
  6. Ech-o, us, *a nymph changed into a sound.*
  7. Electr-a, æ, *daughter of Agamemnon.*
  8. Elysi-um, i, *abode of the pious dead.*
  9. Encelad-us, i, *a giant.*
110. Endymion, is, *a youth beloved by Diana.*
  1. Erechthe-us, i, or os, *king of Athens.*
  2. Erinny-es, um, } *the three Furies, Tisiphon-e, es,*
     Furi-æ, arum, } *Alect-o, us, and Megær-a, æ.*
  3. Europ-a, æ, *sister of Cadmus.*
  4. Eurysthe-us, i, or os, *king of Mycenæ.*
  5. Ganymed-es, is, *son of Priam, cup-bearer of Jupiter.*
  6. Gigant-es, um, *giants, sons of earth.*
  7. Gorgon-es, um, *Medus-a, æ, and her two sisters.*
  8. Grati-æ, arum, } *the three Graces, Aglai-a, æ,*
     Charit-es, um, } *Euphrosyn-e, es, and Thali-a, æ.*
  9. Gyg-es, is, *a giant.*
120. Harpyi-æ, arum, *the Harpies, monstrous and rapacious birds.*
  1. Hector, is, *a Trojan hero, son of Priam.*
  2. Hecub-a, æ, or e, es, *wife of Priam.*
  3. Helen-a, æ, *daughter of Leda, wife of Menelaus and Paris.*
  4. Hercul-es, is, *a hero, son of Jupiter and Alcmena.*
  5. Heraclid-æ, arum, *descendants of Hercules.*
  6. Hippolyt-a, æ, *queen of the Amazones.*
  7. Hippolyt-us, i, *son of Theseus.*
  8. Hypermnestr-a, æ, *one of the daughters of Danaus.*
  9. Icar-us, i, *son of Dædalus.*
130. Idomene-us, i, *king of Crete, a Grecian chief at Troy.*
  1. Inach-us, i, *founder of Argos.*
  2. In-o, us, *daughter of Cadmus.*
  3. I-o, us, *daughter of Inachus.*
  4. Iola-us, i, *cousin and friend of Hercules.*
  5. Iphigeni-a, æ, *daughter of Agamemnon.*
  6. Is-is, idis, *an Egyptian goddess.*

7. Ixi-on, onis, *a king of Thessaly, punished in Tartarus.*
8. Jas-on, onis, *leader of the Argonauts, son of Æs-on, onis.*
9. Jocast-a, æ, *mother of Œdipus.*
140. Laert-es, æ, *father of Ulysses.*
  1. Laocoon, tis, *a Grecian priest at Troy.*
  2. Laodami-a, æ, *wife of Protesilaus.*
  3. Laomedon, tis, *king of Troy, father of Priam.*
  4. Lapith-æ, arum, *a people of Thessaly.*
  5. Latin-us, i, *king of Latium, father of Lavinia.*
  6. Lavini-a, æ, *daughter of Latinus, wife of Æneas.*
  7. Leand-er, ri ; rus, ri, *lover of Hero.*
  8. Led-a, æ, *mother of Castor, Pollux, and Helen.*
  9. Leth-e, es, *a river of Hades.*
150. Lucifer, i, *morning-star.*
  1. Lyca-on, onis, *king of Arcadia.*
  2. Lycurg-us, i, *king of Thrace.*
  3. Macha-on, onis, *Grecian physician, son of Æsculapius.*
  4. Mede-a, æ, *an enchantress, daughter of Æetes.*
  5. Memn-on, onis, *king of Æthiopia, son of Aurora.*
  6. Menela-us, i, *son of Atreus, husband of Helen.*
  7. Mezenti-us, i, *king of Etruria, slain by Æneas.*
  8. Mid-as, æ, *a rich king of Phrygia.*
  9. Mino-s, is, *king of Crete.*
160. Minotaur-us, i, *the Minotaur, a monster.*
  1. Narciss-us, i, *a youth charmed with his own image.*
  2. Neoptolem-us, i, *son of Achilles.*
  3. Nestor, is, *king of Pylos, a Grecian chief at Troy.*
  4. Niob-e, es, *daughter of Tantalus, changed into stone.*
  5. Œdip-us, odis, or i, *king of Thebes, son of Lai-us, i.*
  6. Ogyg-es, is, *an ancient king in Greece.*
  7. Orest-es, æ, and is, *son of Agamemnon.*
  8. Orc-us, i, } *the shades below.*
    Had-es, is, }
  9. Ori-on, onis, *a huntsman changed into a star.*
170. Orphe-us, i, or os, *a Thracian musician.*
  1. Osir-is, idis, *an Egyptian deity.*
  2. Palamed-es, is, *a Grecian chief.*
  3. Pandor-a, æ, *the first woman, sent by Jupiter to Epimetheus.*
  4. Parc-æ, arum, *the Fates, Clotho, Atropos, & Lachesis.*
  5. Par-is, idis, *son of Priam, purloiner of Helen.*
  6. Patrocl-us, i, *friend of Achilles, slain by Hector.*

7. Pegas-us, i, *a winged horse.*
8. Pele-us, i, or os, *husband of Thetis, father of Achilles.*
9. Peli-as, æ, *uncle of Jason.*
180. Pelop-s, is, *son of Tantalus.*
1. Penelop-e, es, *wife of Ulysses.*   [*Cadmus.*
2. Penthe-us, i, or os, *king of Thebes, grandson of*
3. Perse-us, i, or os, *son of Jupiter and Danae.*
4. Phaethon, tis, *son of Sol.*
5. Phalar-is, idis, *a cruel tyrant.*
6. Phædr-a, æ, *wife of Theseus.*
7. Phaon, is, *lover of Sappho.*
8. Philoctet-es, æ, *friend of Hercules.*
9. Philomel-a, æ, *daughter of Pandion, changed into a nightingale.*
190. Phine-us, i, or os, *king of Thrace.*
1. Pic-us, i, *son of Saturn, changed into a woodpecker.*
2. Piritho-us, i, *son of Ixion, friend of Theseus.*
3. Polynic-es, is, *son of Œdipus, brother of Eteocles.*
4. Polyphem-us, i, *a Cyclops.*
5. Priam-us, i, *king of Troy.*
6. Procn-e, es, *sister of Philomela, changed into a swallow.*
7. Promethe-us, i, or os, *son of Iapetus.*
8. Protesila-us, i, *the first Greek who fell at Troy.*
9. Pylad-es, æ, or is, *friend of Orestes.*
200. Python, is, *a serpent killed by Apollo.*
1. Rhadamanth-us, i, *brother of Minos, a judge in Hades.*
2. Rhes-us, i, *a king of Thrace, slain at Troy.*
3. Sarped-on, onis, *a Trojan hero.*
4. Scyll-a, æ, *a dangerous rock on coast of Sicily.*
5. Semel-e, es, *daughter of Cadmus, mother of Bacchus.*
6. Semiram-is, idis, *wife of Ninus, foundress of Babylon.*
7. Sibyll-a, æ, *the Sibyl, a prophetess.*
8. Silen-us, i, *tutor of Bacchus.*
9. Siren-es, um, *musical sorceresses.*
210. Sisyph-us, i, *king of Corinth, punished in Tartarus.*
1. Sphin-x, gis, *a monster.*
2. Sty-x, gis, *a river of Tartarus.*
3. Tantal-us, i, *king of Phrygia, punished in Tartarus.*
4. Tartar-us, i, *the place of infernal punishment.*
5. Telemach-us, i, *son of Ulysses.*
6. Tere-us, i, or os, *king of Thrace.*

7. Teuc-er, ri, *a king of Troy.*
8. Teuc-er, ri, *brother of Ajax, a Grecian chief.*
9. These-us, i, or os, *king of Athens.*
220. Thet-is, idis, *a sea-nymph, mother of Achilles.*
1. Thyest-es, æ, *brother of Atreus.*
2. Tiresi-as, æ, *a Theban seer.*
3. Titan-es, um, *the Titans, sons of Uranus.*
4. Tity-us, i, *a giant.*
5. Triptolem-us, i, *inventer of the plough.*
6. Tro-s, is, *king of Phrygia.*
7. Turn-us, i, *king of the Rutuli.*
8. Tyndar-us, i, *king of Sparta, husband of Leda.*
9. Typhon, is, or Typhœ-us, i, *a giant.*
230. Ulyss-es, is, *king of Ithaca, a Grecian chief at Troy.*

III.—NAMES IN GRECIAN HISTORY.

1. Ag-is, idis, *king of Sparta.*
2. Agesila-us, i, *king of Sparta.*
3. Alcibiad-es, is, *Athenian general.*
4. Alexand-er, ri, *king of Macedonia, conqueror of Asia.*
5. Antigon-us, i, *Macedonian general.*
6. Antioch-us, i, *king of Syria.*
7. Antipat-er, ri, *Macedonian general.*
8. Arat-us, i, *Achæan general.*
9. Aristid-es, is, *Athenian general.*
240. Cambys-es, is, *a king of Persia.*
1. Codr-us, i, *last king of Athens.*
2. Crœsus, i, *a wealthy king of Lydia.*
3. Cyr-us, i, *first king of Persia.*
4. Dari-us, i, *king of Persia.*
5. Draco, nis, *an Athenian legislator.*
6. Dionysi-us, i, *elder and younger, tyrants of Syracuse.*
7. Epaminond-as, æ, *Theban general.*
8. Ephor-i, orum, *Spartan magistrates.*
9. Hiero, nis, *king of Syracuse.*
250. Hippi-as, æ, *tyrant of Athens.*
1. Leonid-as, æ, *king of Sparta.*
2. Lycurg-us, i, *legislator of Sparta.*
3. Lysand-er, ri, *Spartan general.*
4. Miltiad-es, is, *Athenian general.*
5. Pelopid-as, æ, *Theban general.*

H

6. Pericl-es, is, *Athenian statesman and general.*
7. Philipp-us, i, *king of Macedonia, father of Alexander.*
8. Philopœm-en, enis, *Achæan general.*
9. Phocion, is, *Athenian general.*
260. Pisistrat-us, i, *tyrant of Athens.*
1. Ptolemæ-us, i, *king of Egypt.*
2. Seleuc-us, i, *king of Syria.*
3. Sesostr-is, idis, *an ancient king of Egypt.*
4. Themistocl-es, is, *Athenian statesman and general.*
5. Xerx-es, is, *king of Persia.*

IV.—NAMES IN GRECIAN LITERATURE AND ART.

6. Æschin-es, is, *orator.*
7. Æschyl-us, i, *tragic poet.*
8. Æsop-us, i, *fabulist.*
9. Alcæ-us, i, *lyric poet.*
270. Anacreon, tis, *lyric poet.*
1. Apell-es, is, *painter.*
2. Aristophan-es, is, *comic poet.*
3. Aristotel-es, is, *philosopher.*
4. Bion, is, *pastoral poet.*
5. Callimach-us, i, *elegiac poet.*
6. Demosthen-es, is, *orator.*
7. Epicur-us, i, *philosopher.*
8. Euclid-es, is, *mathematician.*
9. Euripid-es, is, *tragic poet.*
280. Herodot-us, i, *historian.*
1. Hesiod-us, i, *didactic poet.*
2. Hippocrat-es, is, *physician.*
3. Homer-us, i, *epic poet.*
4. Isocrat-es, is, *orator.*
5. Lysi-as, æ, *orator.*
6. Lysipp-us, i, *sculptor.*
7. Mosch-us, i, *pastoral poet.*
8. Parrhasi-us, i, *painter.*
9. Phidi-as, æ, *sculptor.*
290. Pindar-us, i, *lyric poet.*
1. Plato, nis, *philosopher.*
2. Plutarch-us, i, *biographer.*
3. Polybi-us, i, *historian.*
4. Polyclet-us, i, *sculptor.*

5. Praxitel-es, is, *sculptor.*
6. Pythagor-as, æ, *philosopher.*
7. Sapph-o, us, *lyric poetess.*
8. Simonid-es, is, *lyric poet.*
9. Socrat-es, is, *philosopher.*
300. Solon, is, *legislator, philosopher, and poet.*
  1. Sophocl-es, is, *tragic poet.*
  2. Strabo, nis, *geographer.*
  3. Thal-es, is, or etis, *philosopher.*
  4. Theocrit-us, i, *pastoral poet.*
  5. Theophrast-us, i, *philosopher and naturalist.*
  6. Thucydid-es, is, *historian.*
  7. Tyrtæ-us, i, *elegiac poet.*
  8. Xenophon, tis, *historian.*
  9. Zeux-is, idis, *painter.*

V.—NAMES IN ROMAN HISTORY.

310. Æmili-us, i, (1) *Consul killed at Cannæ*, (2) *Consul who conquered Macedonia.*
  1. Agricol-a, æ, *general who conquered Britain.*
  2. Agripp-a, æ, *general.*
  3. Amuli-us, i, *king of Alba, brother of Numitor.*
  4. Anc-us, i, *fourth king of Rome.*
  5. Antonin-us, i, *emperor.*
  6. Antoni-us, i, (1) *an orator*, (2) *the triumvir defeated at Actium.*
  7. Appi-us, i, *a name common to many famous Romans.*
  8. Attal-us, i, *king of Pergamus.*
  9. August-us, i, *the first Roman emperor.*
320. Aureli-us, i, *emperor.*
  1. Brut-us, i, (1) *expeller of Tarquin*, (2) *conspirator against J. Cæsar.*
  2. Cæsar, is, (C. Julius), *the Dictator, slain in the senate-house.*
  3. Caligul-a, æ, *third emperor.*
  4. Camill-us, i, *a famous general.*
  5. Cassi-us, i, *conspirator against Cæsar.*
  6. Catilin-a, æ, *conspirator against the Republic, killed in battle.*
  7. Cato, nis, (1) *the Censor*, (2) *the Stoic, killed himself at Utica.*

8. Cincinnat-us, i, *victorious general.*

9. Claudi-us, i, *fourth emperor.*

330. Cleopatr-a, æ, *queen of Egypt.*

1. Constantin-us, i, *first Christian emperor.*

2. Coriolan-us, i, *a victorious general, banished.*

3. Crass-us, i, (1) *an orator;* (2) *the rich triumvir,
slain by the Parthians.*

4. Curti-us, i, *a Roman who leapt into the gulph.*

5. Curi-us, i, (Dentatus) *a victorious general.*

6. Deci-us, i, *several of this name devoted themselves
to death for their country.*

7. Drus-us, i, *stepson of Augustus.*

8. Fabi-us, i, *a general who baffled Hannibal.*

9. Fabrici-us, i, *a successful general and upright man.*

340. Flaminin-us, i, (1) *Consul killed at lake Trasymenus;*
(2) *Consul victorious against Philip of Macedon.*

1. Galb-a, æ, *emperor.*

2. Gracch-us, i, *Tiberius and Caius, both slain while
attempting to weaken the power of the senate.*

3. Hadrian-us, i, *emperor.*

4. Hannibal, is, *a great Carthaginian general.*

5. Hasdrubal, is, *brother of Hannibal, killed in battle.*

6. Hostili-us, i, (Tullus) *third king of Rome.*

7. Jub-a, æ, *king of Mauritania.*

8. Jugurth-a, æ, *king of Numidia, conquered by Marius.*

9. Lepid-us, i, *triumvir with Augustus and Antony.*

350. Lentul-us, i, *name of a Patrician family at Rome.*

1. Lucull-us, i, *successful general against Mithridates.*

2. Mæcen-as, atis, *minister of Augustus.*

3. Manli-us, i, *preserver of the Capitol from the Gauls.*

4. Mari-us, i, *a successful general, rival of Sulla.*

5. Marcell-us, i, *conqueror of Syracuse.*

6. Masiniss-a, æ, *king of Numidia.*

7. Metell-us, i, *a successful general.*

8. Mithridat-es, is, *king of Pontus.*

9. Nero, nis, *a wicked emperor.*

360. Nerv-a, æ, *emperor.*

1. Num-a, æ, *second king of Rome.*

2. Numit-or, oris, *grandfather of Romulus.*

3. Otho, nis, *emperor.*

4. Piso, nis, *the name of an eminent family.*

5. Pompei-us, i, *the triumvir, murdered in Egypt.*

6. Porsen-a, æ, *king of Etruria.*
7. Quirit-es, ium, *the Romans.*
8. Regul-us, i, *an eminent general, put to death at Carthage.*
9. Rem-us, i, *brother of Romulus.*
370. Romul-us, i, *founder of Rome.*
1. Scipi-o, nis, (1) *conqueror of Hannibal,* (2) *destroyer of Carthage.*
2. Semproni-us, i, *Consul defeated by Hannibal.*
3. Servi-us, i, (Tulli-us, i,) *sixth king of Rome.*
4. Sull-a, æ, *a successful general, rival of Marius.*
5. Syph-ax, acis, *king of Numidia.*
6. Tarquini-us, (1) *fifth king of Rome,* (2) *seventh and last king of Rome.*
7. Tiberi-us, i, *second emperor.*
8. Trajan-us, i, *emperor.*
9. Vespasian-us, i, *emperor.*
380. Vitelli-us, i, *emperor.*

VI.—NAMES IN ROMAN LITERATURE.

1. Ausoni-us, i, *poet.*
2. Catull-us, i, *lyric poet.*
3. Cels-us, i, *physician.*
4. Cicero, nis, *statesman, orator, and philosopher.*
5. Claudian-us, i, *epic poet.*
6. Enni-us, i, *epic poet.*
7. Horati-us, i, *lyric and satiric poet.*
8. Justin-us, i, *historian.*
9. Juvenal-is, is, *satiric poet.*
390. Livi-us, i, *historian.*
1. Lucan-us, i, *epic poet.*
2. Lucili-us, i, *satiric poet.*
3. Lucreti-us, i, *didactic poet.*
4. Martial-is, is, *epigrammatic poet.*
5. Nep-os, otis, *biographer.*
6. Ovidi-us, i, *elegiac poet.*
7. Persi-us, i, *satiric poet.*
8. Phædr-us, i, *fabulist.*
9. Plaut-us, i, *comic poet.*
400. Plini-us, i, *naturalist.*
1. Properti-us, i, *elegiac poet.*

H 3

2. Quintilian-us, i, *rhetorician.*
3. Rosci-us, i, *actor.*
4. Sallusti-us, i, *historian.*
5. Senec-a, æ, (1) *philosopher*, (2) *tragic poet.*
6. Sili-us, i, *epic poet.*
7. Stati-us, i, *epic poet.*
8. Suetoni-us, i, *biographer.*
9. Tacit-us, i, *historian.*
410. Terenti-us, i, *comic poet.*
1. Tibull-us, i, *elegiac poet.*
2. Valeri-us, i, *epic poet.*
3. Varro, nis, *agriculturist and grammarian.*
4. Vitruvi-us, i, *architect.*
5. Virgili-us, i, *epic, didactic, and pastoral poet.*

VII.—NATIONAL NAMES.

6. Acarnan, is, *Acarnanian.*
7. Achiv-us, a, um,
Achæ-us, a, um,
Dana-us, a, um,
Græc-us, a, um, } *Grecian.*
Grai-us, a, um,
Pelasg-us, a, um,
8. Æol-es, um, *Æolians.*
9. Æthiop-s, is, *Ethiopian.*
420. Ætol-us, a, um, *Ætolian.*
1. Af-er, ra, rum, *African.*
2. Appul-us, a, um, *Apulian.*
3. Arab-s, is, *Arabian.*
4. Arc-as, adis, *Arcadian.*
5. Argiv-us, a, um, *Argive, or Grecian.*
6. Atheniens-is, e, *Athenian.*
7. Britann-us, a, um, *Briton.*
8. Calab-er, ra, rum, *Calabrian.*
9. Carthaginiens-is, e,
Pœn-us, a, um, } *Carthaginian.*
Punic-us, a, um,
430. Cil-ix, icis, *Cilician.*
1. Dor-es, um, *Dorians.*
2. Gall-us, a, um, *Gaul, Gaulish.*
3. German-us, a, um, *German.*

4. Hispaniens-is, e, ⎫
   Iber, a, um,   ⎬ *Spaniard, Spanish.*
5. Ind-us, a, um, *Indian.*
6. Ion-es, um, *Jonians.*
7. Ital-us, a, um, *Italian.*
8. Ithac-us, a, um, *Ithacan.*
9. Judæ-us, a, um, *Jew, Jewish.*
440. Lacedæmoni-us, a, um, *Lacedæmonian.*
1. Latin-us, a, um, *Latian, Latin.*
2. Ligur, is, *Ligurian.*
3. Maced-o, onis, *Macedonian.*
4. Mars-us, a, um, *Marsian.*
5. Med-us, a, um, *Mede, Median.*
6. Pers-a, æ, *Persian.*
7. Phry-x, gis, *Phrygian.*
8. Roman-us, a, um, *Roman.*
9. Sabin-us, a, um, *Sabine.*
450. Samn-is, itis, *Samnite.*
1. Sarmat-a, æ, *Sarmatian.*
2. Scyth-a, æ, *Scythian.*
3. Sicul-us, a, um, ⎫
   Sican-us, a, um, ⎬ *Sicilian.*
   Siciliens-is, e, ⎭
4. Syr-us, a, um, *Syrian.*
5. Theban-us, a, um, *Theban.*
6. Thessal-us, a, um, *Thessalian.*
7. Thra-x, cis, *Thracian.*
8. Tro-s, is,   ⎫
   Trojan-us, a, um, ⎬ *Trojan.*
9. Tusc-us, a, um,   ⎫
   Tyrrhen-us, a, um, ⎬ *Tuscan.*

VIII.—NAMES OF CONTINENTS.

460. Afric-a. æ, *Africa.*
1. Asi-a, æ, *Asia.*
2. Europ-a, æ, *Europe.*

IX.—NAMES OF COUNTRIES.

3. Ægypt-us, i, *Egypt, in Africa.*
4. Æthiopi-a, æ, *Ethiopia, in Africa.*

5. Arabi-a, æ, *Arabia, in Asia.*
6. Armeni-a, æ, *Armenia, in Asia.*
7. Assyri-a, æ, *Assyria, in Asia.*
8. Bithyni-a, æ, *in Asia.*
9. Britanni-a, æ, *Britain, European island.*
470. Cappadoci-a, æ, *in Asia.*
 1. Cari-a, æ, *in Asia.*
 2. Chaldæ-a, æ, *in Asia.*
 3. Cilici-a, æ, *in Asia.*
 4. Colch-is, idis, *in Asia.*
 5. Daci-a, æ, *in Europe.*
 6. Epir-us, i, *in Europe.*
 7. Galati-a, æ, *in Asia.*
 8. Galli-a, æ, *Gaul, in Europe.*
 9. Germani-a, æ, *Germany, in Europe.*
480. Græci-a, æ, *Greece, in Europe.*
 1. Hispani-a, æ, *Spain, in Europe.*
 2. Indi-a, æ, *in Asia.*
 3. Itali-a, æ, *Italy, in Europe.*
 4. Liby-a, æ, *in Africa.*
 5. Lusitani-a, æ, *Portugal, in Europe.*
 6. Lyci-a, æ, *in Asia.*
 7. Lydi-a, æ, *in Asia.*
 8. Macedoni-a, æ, *in Europe.*
 9. Mauritani-a, æ, *in Africa.*
490. Medi-a, æ, *in Asia.*
 1. Mesopotami-a, æ, *in Asia.*
 2. Mœsi-a, æ, *in Europe.*
 3. Mysi-a, æ, *in Asia.*
 4. Noric-um, i, *in Europe.*
 5. Numidi-a, æ, *in Africa.*
 6. Palæstin-a, æ, *Palestine, in Asia.*
 7. Pamphyli-a, æ, *in Asia.*
 8. Paphlagoni-a, æ, *in Asia.*
 9. Pannoni-a, æ, *in Europe.*
500. Parthi-a, æ, *in Asia.*
 1. Pers-is, idis, *Persia, in Asia.*
 2. Phœnic-e, es, or Phœnici-a, æ, *in Asia.*
 3. Phrygi-a, æ, *in Asia.*
 4. Pont-us, i, *in Asia.*
 5. Rhæti-a, æ, *in Europe.*
 6. Sarmati-a, æ, *in Europe and Asia.*

7. Scandinavi-a, æ, *in Europe.*
8. Scythi-a, æ, *in Europe and Asia.*
9. Syri-a, æ, *in Asia.*
510. Thraci-a, æ, *Thrace, in Europe.*
1. Vindelici-a, æ, *in Europe.*

X.—NAMES OF DISTRICTS, PROVINCES, ISLANDS.

2. Acarnani-a, æ, *in Greece.*
3. Achai-a, æ, *in Greece.*
4. Ægin-a, æ, *Grecian island.*
5. Æoli-a, æ, *in Mysia.*
6. Ætoli-a, æ, *in Greece.*
7. Apuli-a, æ, *in Italy.*
8. Arcadi-a, æ, *in Greece.*
9. Argol-is, idis, *in Greece.*
520. Attic-a, æ, *in Greece.*
1. Bœoti-a, æ, *in Greece.*
2. Campani-a, æ, *in Italy.*
3. Chi-os, i, *Grecian island.*
4. Corcyr-a, æ, *Grecian island.*
5. Corsic-a, æ, *Italian island.*
6. Cret-a, æ, *Grecian island.*
7. Cyclad-es, um, *Grecian islands.*
8. Cypr-us, i, *Grecian island.*
9. Cyther-a, orum, *Grecian island.*
530. Del-os, i, *Grecian island.*
1. Dor-is, idis, (1) *in Greece,* (2) *in Caria.*
2. El-is, idis, *in Greece.*
3. Emathi-a, æ, *in Greece and Macedonia.*
4. Etruri-a, æ, *in Italy.*
5. Eubœ-a, æ, *Grecian island.*
6. Ioni-a, æ, *in Lydia.*
7. Ithac-a, æ, *Grecian island.*
8. Judæ-a, æ, *in Palestine.*
9. Laconi-a, æ, *in Greece.*
540. Lati-um, i, *in Italy.*
1. Lemn-os, i, *Grecian island.*
2. Lesb-os, i, *Grecian island.*
3. Locr-is, idis, *in Greece.*
4. Lucani-a, æ, *in Italy.*
5. Messeni-a, æ, *in Greece.*

6. Nax-os, i, *Grecian island.*
7. Par-os, i, *Grecian island.*
8. Patm-os, i, *Grecian island.*
9. Peloponnes-us, i, *the southern part of Greece.*
550. Phoc-is, idis, *in Greece.*
 1. Phthi-a, æ, *in Thessaly, (Greece).*
 2. Pieri-a, æ, *in Macedonia.*
 3. Pæoni-a, æ, *in Macedonia.*
 4. Rhod-us, i, *Rhodes, Grecian island.*
 5. Salam-is, inis, *Grecian island.*
 6. Sam-os, i, *Grecian island.*
 7. Sardini-a, æ, *Italian island.*
 8. Sicili-a, æ, *the island of Sicily.*
 9. Tened-os, i, *Grecian island.*
560. Thessali-a, æ, *Thessaly, in Greece.*

XI.—NAMES OF CITIES, TOWNS, &c.

 1. Abyd-os, i, *in Mysia.*
 2. Academi-a, æ, *the* ACADEMY, *at Athens.*
 3. Acti-um, i, *in Epirus.*
 4. Alexandri-a, æ, *in Egypt.*
 5. Antiochi-a, æ, *Antioch, in Syria.*
 6. Arbel-a, orum, *in Assyria.*
 7. Arg-os, i, or Arg-i, orum, *in Argolis.*
 8. Arpin-um, i, *in Italy.*
 9. Athen-æ, arum, *Athens, in Attica.*
570. Aul-is, idis, *in Bœotia.*
 1. Babylon, is, *in Chaldæa.*
 2. Brundisi-um, i, *in Italy.*
 3. Byzanti-um, i, afterwards Constantinopolis, is, } *in Thrace.*
 4. Calp-e, es, *in Spain.*
 5. Cann-æ, arum, *in Italy.*
 6. Capu-a, æ, *in Campania, (Italy).*
 7. Carthag-o, inis, *Carthage, in Africa.*
 8. Chærone-a, æ, *in Bœotia.*
 9. Cnid-us, i, *in Caria.*
580. Corinth-us, i, *Corinth, in Peloponnesus.*
 1. Cyren-e, es, *in Libya.*
 2. Damasc-us, i, *in Syria.*
 3. Delph-i, orum, *in Phocis.*

4. Dodon-a, æ, *in Epirus.*
5. Eleus-is, inis, *in Attica.*
6. Ephes-us, i, *in Jonia.*
7. Halicarnass-us, i, *in Caria.*
8. Hierosolum-æ, arum, *(Jerusalem) in Palestine.*
9. Idali-um, i, *in Cyprus.*
590. Iolc-us, i, *in Thessaly.*
1. Ips-us, i, *in Phrygia.*
2. Iss-us, i, *in Cilicia.*
3. Lacedæm-on, onis, } *in Laconia.*
   Spart-a, æ, }
4. Lariss-a, æ, *in Thessaly.*
5. Leuctr-a, orum, *in Bœotia.*
6. Londini-um, i, *(London) in Britain.*
7. Lugdun-um, i, *in Gaul.*
8. Luteti-a, æ, *(Paris) in Gaul.*
9. Mantine-a, æ, *in Arcadia.*
600. Mantu-a, æ, *in Italy.*
1. Marathon, is, *in Attica.*
2. Massili-a, æ, *(Marseilles) in Gaul.*
3. Megar-a, orum, *in Greece.*
4. Memph-is, idis, *in Egypt.*
5. Milet-us, i, *in Jonia.*
6. Mutin-a, æ, *in Italy.*
7. Mycen-æ, arum, *in Argolis.*
8. Neme-a, æ, *in Argolis.*
9. Numanti-a, æ, *in Spain.*
610. Olympi-a, æ, *in Elis.*
1. Olynth-us, i, *in Macedonia.*
2. Orchomen-us, i, *in Bœotia.*
3. Palmyr-a, æ, *in Syria.*
4. Paph-os, i, *in Cyprus.*
5. Pell-a, æ, *in Macedonia.*
6. Persepol-is, is, *in Persia.*
7. Pergam-us, i, *in Mysia.*
8. Pharsal-us, i, *in Thessaly.*
9. Philipp-i, orum, *in Thrace.*
620. Pis-a, æ, *in Elis.*
1. Piræ-us, i, *the port of Athens.*
2. Platæ-æ, arum, *in Bœotia.*
3. Potidæ-a, æ, *in Macedonia.*
4. Prænest-e, is, *in Latium.*

5. Pydn-a, æ, *in Macedonia.*
6. Pyl-os, i, *in Peloponnesus.*
7. Rom-a, æ, *in Latium.*
8. Sard-es, ium, *in Lydia.*
9. Sidon, is, *in Phœnicia.*
630. Sicyon, is, *in Peloponnesus.*
1. Smyrn-a, æ, *in Jonia.*
2. Syracus-æ, arum, *in Sicily.*
3. Tarent-um, i, *in Italy.*
4. Tars-us, i, *in Cilicia.*
5. Tempe, *a vale in Thessaly.*
6. Theb-æ, arum, (1) *in Bœotia, having 7 gates,*
   (2) *in Egypt, having 100 gates.*
7. Thermopyl-æ, arum, *in Locris.*
8. Tibur, is, *in Italy.*
9. Troj-a, æ, }
   Ili-um, i, } *(Troy) in Mysia.*
640. Tyr-us, i, *(Tyre) in Phœnicia.*
1. Vei-i, orum, *in Etruria.*
2. Veron-a, æ, *in Italy.*

XII.—NAMES OF MOUNTAINS.

3. Ætn-a, æ, *in Sicily.*
4. Alp-es, ium, *bounding Italy on the north.*
5. Anchesm-us, i, *in Attica.*
6. Ath-os, o, *in Macedonia.*
7. Apennin-us, i, *in Italy.*
8. Atl-as, antis, *in Mauritania.*
9. Caucas-us, i, *in Asia.*
650. Cithæron, is, *in Bœotia.*
1. Crag-us, i, *in Lycia.*
2. Cyllen-e, es, *in Arcadia.*
3. Cynth-us, i, *in Delos.*
4. Dict-e, es, *in Crete.*
5. Dindym-us, i, *in Phrygia.*
6. Erymanth-us, i, *in Arcadia.*
7. Ery-x, cis, *in Sicily.*
8. Hæm-us, i, *in Thrace.*
9. Helicon, is, *in Bœotia.*
660. Hybl-a, æ, *in Sicily.*
1. Hymett-us, i, *in Attica.*

2. Id-a, æ, (1) *in Mysia*, (2) *in Crete.*
3. Ismar-us, i, *in Thrace.*
4. Latm-us, i, *in Caria.*
5. Lycæ-us, i, *in Arcadia.*
6. Mænal-us, i, *in Arcadia.*
7. Mycal-e, es, *in Ionia.*
8. Niphat-es, is, *in Armenia.*
9. Œt-a, æ, *in Thessaly.*
670. Olymp-us, i, (1) *in Macedonia*, (2) *in Bithynia.*
1. Oss-a, æ, *in Thessaly.*
2. Othry-s, os, *in Thessaly.*
3. Parnass-us, i, *in Phocis.*
4. Peli-on, i, *in Thessaly.*
5. Pentelic-us, i, *in Attica.*
6. Pind-us, i, *in Thessaly.*
7. Pyrenæ-i, orum, *between Gaul and Spain.*
8. Rhodop-e, es, *in Thrace.*
9. Tænar-us, i, *in Laconia.*
680. Taur-us, i, *in Asia.*
1. Tayget-us, i, *in Laconia.*
2. Tmol-us, i, *in Lydia.*
3. Vesuvi-us, i, *in Italy.*

XIII.—NAMES OF RIVERS.

4. Achelo-us, i, *in Acarnania.*
5. Alli-a, æ, *in Italy.*
6. Alphe-us, i, *in Elis.*
7. Amphrys-us, i, *in Thessaly.*
8. Athes-is, is, *(Adige) in Italy.*
9. Aufid-us, i, *in Italy.*
690. Caystr-us, i, *in Lydia.*
1. Cephis-us, i, (1) *in Attica*, (2) *in Bœotia.*
2. Danubi-us, i, } *(Danube) in Europe.*
   Ist-er, ri, }
3. Even-us, i, *in Ætolia.*
4. Euphrat-es, is, *in Asia.*
5. Eurot-as, æ, *in Laconia.*
6. Gang-es, is, *in India.*
7. Granic-us, i, *in Mysia.*
8. Hebr-us, i, *in Thrace.*
9. Iliss-us, i, *in Attica.*

I

700. Mæand-er, ri, *in Caria.*
  1. Minci-us, i, *in Italy.*
  2. Nar, is, *in Italy.*
  3. Nil-us, i, *in Egypt.*
  4. Pad-us, i, or Eridan-us, i, *(Po) in Italy.*
  5. Pactol-us, i, *in Lydia.*
  6. Pene-us, i, *in Thessaly.*
  7. Phas-is, idis, *in Colchis.*
  8. Rhen-us, i, *(Rhine) in Europe.*
  9. Rhodan-us, i, *(Rhone) in Gaul.*
710. Rubico, nis, *in Italy.*
  1. Sabrin-a, æ, *(Severn) in Britain.*
  2. Scamand-er, ri, *in Mysia.*
  3. Simo-is, entis, *in Mysia.*
  4. Sperchi-us, i, *in Thessaly.*
  5. Strym-on, onis, *in Macedonia.*
  6. Tag-us, i, *in Spain.*
  7. Tames-is, is, *(Thames) in Britain.*
  8. Tana-is, is, *(Don) in Sarmatia.*
  9. Thermodon, tis, *in Pontus.*
720. Tiber-is, is, or Tybr-is, idis, *in Italy.*
  1. Ticin-us, i, *in Italy.*
  2. Trebi-a, æ, *in Italy.*

WINDS.

  3. Afric-us, i, *South-west wind.*
  4. Apeliot-es, æ, *East wind.*
  5. Aquilo, nis, } *North wind.*
  6. Bore-as, æ, }
  7. Aust-er, ri, } *South wind.*
  8. Not-us, i, }
  9. Caur-us, i, *North-east wind.*
730. Favoni-us, i, } *West wind.*
  1. Zephyr-us, i, }

EXERCISES ON THE VOCABULARY.

EXERCISE I.

A. As the Master reads the Latin Words in a Section, the boys repeat the English.

B. As the Master reads the English Words, the boys repeat the Latin.

C. The boys repeat the whole Section, Latin with English, from memory.

EXERCISE II.

The boys analyze (or parse) the Words of a Section, as follows:—

A.   ( ) is a Substantive
            of the (   ) Declension,
                   (   ) Gender,
            declined like (   )

Here let it be declined. And let Rule for Gender be repeated.

If the Substantive is Irregular, the boys will say: (   ) is an Irregular Substantive, &c.

B.   ( ) is an Adjective
            of ( ) Terminations,
            declined like (   )

Here let it be declined.

            compared $\left\{ \begin{array}{c} \text{regularly} \\ \text{or} \\ \text{irregularly} \end{array} \right\}$

Here let it be compared.

C.   ( ) is a ( ) Pronoun.

Here let it be declined.

D.   ( ) is a Verb $\left\{ \begin{array}{c} \text{Active} \\ \text{or} \\ \text{Deponent} \end{array} \right\}$
            of the ( ) Conjugation.

Here let it be conjugated.

Its Preterperfect and Supine are formed by Rule ( )

If the Verb is Irregular, Defective, or Impersonal, the boy must state so before the word Verb: as, Aio is a Defective Verb Active, &c.

E.   ( ) is an Adverb.
F.   ( ) is a Preposition.
G.   ( ) is a Conjunction.
H.   ( ) is an Interjection.

———

Example.—The boys, having said the first 9 words (a - - - ad) in the way shown in Exercise I., open their books and go on thus:

1. A or ab is a Preposition.

2. Abies, is a Substantive
        of the 3rd Declension,
        ,,   ,, Feminine Gender,

   declined like { }

Here the boy will name the Example in his Latin Grammar, like which abies is declined.

	Sing.	Plur.
Nom.	abies, *a fir-tree*	abietes, *fir-trees*
Gen.	abiĕtis, *of a fir-tree*	abietum, *of fir-trees*
Dat.	abieti, *to a fir-tree*	abietibus, *to fir-trees*
Acc.	abietem, *a fir-tree*	abietes, *fir-trees*
Voc.	abies, *O fir-tree*	abietes, *O fir-trees*
Abl.	abiete, *by, with, or from a fir-tree.*	abietibus, *by, with, or from fir-trees.*

Rule for Gender, is ( )

Here the boy will repeat the Rule for Gender from his Latin Grammar.

3. Ac, atque, are Conjunctions.

4. Accipiter, is a Substantive
        of the 3rd Declension,
        ,, ,, Masculine Gender.
        declined like nubes (except Gen. Plur.)
   Here the Rule for Gen. Plural may be given.

	Sing.		Plur.
Nom.	accipiter, *a hawk*		accipitres, *hawks*
Gen.	accipitris, *of a hawk*		accipitrum, *of hawks*
Dat.	accipitri, *to a hawk*		accipitribus, *to hawks*
Acc.	accipitrem, *a hawk*		accipitres, *hawks*
Voc.	accipiter, *O hawk*		accipitres, *O hawks*
Abl.	accipitre, *by, with, or from a hawk.*		accipitribus, *by, with, or from hawks.*

Rule for Gender, is ( )

Here the boy will repeat the Rule for Gender from his Latin Grammar.

5. Aceo, is a Verb Active
of the 2nd Conjugation.

Aceo, aces, acui, acere, acendi, acendo, acendum, acens : no Supines.

Its Preterperfect is formed by Rule ( )

Here Rule for Preterperfect must be repeated from the Latin Grammar.

Rule for Defect of Supines, is ( )

Here Rule for Defect of Supines must be given from the Latin Grammar.

6. Acerbus, is an Adjective
of 3 Terminations,
declined like bonus.

	Sing.		Plur.
Nom.	Acerbus, acerba, acerbum,		acerbi, acerbæ, acerba, [rum,
Gen.	acerbi, acerbæ, acerbi,		acerborum, acerbarum, acerbo-
Dat.	acerbo, acerbæ, acerbo,		acerbis, acerbis, acerbis,
Acc.	acerbum, acerbam, acerbum,		acerbos, acerbas, acerba,
Voc.	acerbe, acerba, acerbum,		acerbi, acerbæ, acerba,
Abl.	acerbo, acerba, acerbo,		acerbis, acerbis, acerbis.

Compared regularly,
acerbus, acerbior, acerbissimus.

7. Acervus, is a Substantive
of the 2nd Declension,
„ „ Masculine Gender
declined like dominus.

13

Sing.	Plur.
Nom. Acervus, *a heap*	Acervi, *heaps*
Gen. Acervi, *of a heap*	acervorum, *of heaps*
Dat. Acervo, *to a heap*	acervis, *to heaps*
Acc. Acervum, *a heap*	acervos, *heaps*
Voc. Acerve, *O heap*	acervi, *O heaps*
Abl. Acervo, *by, with, or from a heap.*	acervis, *by, with, or from heaps.*

Rule for Gender, is ( )

Here the boy will repeat the Rule for Gender from his Latin Grammar.

8. Acuo, is a Verb Active
of the 3rd Conjugation.

Acuo, acuis, acui, acuĕre, acuendi, acuendo, acuendum, acutum, acutu, acuens, acuturus.

Its Preterperfect and Supines are formed by Rule ( )

Here Rule for Preterperfect and Supine must be repeated from the Latin Grammar.

9. Ad, is a Preposition.

N.B. This Exercise may be variously done. Sometimes one boy may parse an *entire* section. Sometimes the boys in class may each parse a word. At other times the answering may pass rapidly through the class, each boy giving one fact, case, rule, &c. only. Thus acervus, so parsed, will afford answers for 17 boys. Sometimes the Exercise may be required in writing.

EXERCISE III.

Any portion of the Vocabulary being appointed, the boys will classify the words in the following manner.

This portion contains

A.   ( ) Substantives; of which
  a.   ( ) are of the 1st Declension; namely......
  b.   ( ) „ „ „ 2nd „ „ „ ......
  c.   ( ) „ „ „ 3rd „ „ „ ......
  d.   ( ) „ „ „ 4th „ „ „ ......
  e.   ( ) „ „ „ 5th „ „ „ ......
     ( ) are Defective, namely........
  (a)   ( ) „ Masculine, „ ....
  (b)   ( ) „ Feminine, „ ....
  (c)   ( ) „ Neuter, „ ....

B. ( ) Adjectives; of which
    a. ( ) are of 3 Terminations, like bonus, namely..
    b. ( )   ,,   ,,   ,,   ,,   tener   ,,   ..
    c. ( )   ,,   ,,   ,,   ,,   niger   ,,   ..
    d. ( )   ,,   ,,   ,,   ,,   acer   ,,   ..
    c. ( )   ,, 2 ,,   ,,   ,,   tristis   ,,   ..
    f. ( )   ,, 1 ,,   ,,   ,,   felix   ,,   ..

C. ( ) Pronouns; namely........

D. ( ) Verbs; of which
    a. ( ) are of the 1st Conjugation, namely......
    b. ( )   ,,   2nd ,,   ,,   ,, ...
    c. ( )   ,,   3rd ,,   ,,   ,, ...
    d. ( )   ,,   4th ,,   ,,   ,, ...
   (A) ( ) are Active; namely........
   (B) ( ) ,, Deponent ,, ...
   (a) ( ) ,, Irregular ,, ...
   (b) ( ) ,, Defective ,, ...

E. ( ) Adverbs; namely ....

F. ( ) Prepositions ,, ...

G. ( ) Conjunctions ,, ...

H. ( ) Interjections ,, ...

EXERCISE IV.

Write down

A. *a.* ( ) Fem. Substantives of the 1st Declension,
    b. ( ) Masc.   ,,   ,,   ,,   ,,   ,,
B. *a.* (·) Masc.   ,,   ,,   ,, 2nd ,, like dominus.
    b. ( ) Fem.   ,,   ,,   ,,   ,,   ,,
    c. ( ) Masc.   ,,   ,,   ,,   ,,   magister.
    d. ( )   ,,   ,,   ,,   ,,   ,,   puer.
    e. ( ) Neut.   ,,   ,,   ,,   ,,
C. *(a)* ( ) Fem. Parisyllables of the 3rd Declension, in *es.*
   (b) ( ) Masc.   ,,   ,,   ,,   ,,   ,,   ,,
   (c) ( ) Fem.   ,,   ,,   ,,   ,,   ,,   *is.*
   (d) ( ) Masc.   ,,   ,,   ,,   ,,   ,,   ,,
   (e) ( ) Masc.   ,,   ,,   ,,   ,,   ,,   *er.*
   (f) ( ) Fem.   ,,   ,,   ,,   ,,   ,,   ,,
   (g) ( ) Neut.   ,,   ,,   ,,   ,,   ,,   *e.*

104

b. Imparisyllables of the 3rd Declension:

( ) Neut. in *a:* ( ) Masc. in *o:* ( ) Fem. in *o:*
( ) Masc. in *l:* ( ) Neut. in *l:* ( ) Masc. in *n:*
( ) Fem. in *n:* ( ) Neut. in *n:* ( ) Neut. in *ar:*
( ) Masc. in *er:* ( ) Fem. in *er:* ( ) Neut. in *er:*
( ) Masc. in *or:* ( ) Fem. in *or:* ( ) Neut. in *or:*
( ) Masc. in *ur:* ( ) Neut. in *ur:* ( ) Masc. in *as:*
( ) Fem. in *as:* ( ) Neut. in *as:* ( ) Masc. in *es:*
( ) Fem. in *es:* ( ) Masc. in *is;* ( ) Fem. in *is:*
( ) Masc. in *os:* ( ) Fem. in *os:* ( ) Neut. in *os:*
( ) Masc. in *us:* ( ) Fem. in *us:* ( ) Neut. in *us:*
( ) Fem. in *ans:* ( ) Masc. in *ns, ps:* ( ) Fem. in
bs, ps, ms, ls, ns, rs: ( ) Fem. in *ax:* ( ) Masc. in
ex: ( ) Fem. in *ex:* ( ) Masc. in *ix:* ( ) Fem. in
ix: ( ) Fem. in *ox:* ( ) Fem. in *ux:* ( ) Masc. in
yx: ( ) Fem. in *yx:* ( ) Fem. in *lx, nx, rx.*

D. *a.* ( ) Masc. Subst. of the 4th Decl. like *gradus.*
   b. ( ) Fem. ,, ,, ,, ,, ,, ,,

E. ( ) Fem. ,, ,, 5th ,, ,, *facies.*

N.B. Let the Genitive of each word be written down as well as the Nominative, and the Rule for Gender be given.

A. Write down ( ) Substantives of common Gender
     a. in 1st Declension.
     b. ,, 2nd ,,
     c. ,, 3rd ,,

B. Write down ( ) Substantives
   a. Wanting the Singular Number:
     (*a*) in the 1st Declension.
     (*b*) ,, 2nd ,,
     (*c*) ,, 3rd ,,
     (*d*) ,, 4th ,,
   b. Wanting the Plural Number.
c. Wanting some cases: and write down those they have.
d. Redundant in Declension: and decline them fully.

OBSERVATIONS.

Obs. I.—A. Nouns Substantive, which distinguish individuals from others of the same class, are called Proper Names: as, *Alexander, Bucephalus, Babylon, Euphrates.*

Proper Names may be

    Personal, as, names of deities, men, women, &c.

    Local, as, names of countries, towns, mountains, rivers, &c.

B. Appellatives, or Common Names, are Nouns Substantive, which belong to many individuals in common, as, *man, horse, city, river.*

Common Names may be variously classified: as,

    Names of Persons, as, *man, king, boy, painter, &c.*

    Names of Animals, as, *lion, eagle, whale, gnat, &c.*

    Names of Plants, as, *oak, rose, lily, parsley, &c.*

    Names of Constructed Objects, as, *house, ship, knife, &c.*

    Material Names, or names of natural substances, as, *earth, air, gold, wool, &c.*

    Partitive Names, expressing a part of something, as, *face, skin, leaf, root, &c.*

    Collective Names, or Nouns of Multitude, expressing an assemblage, as, *people, flock, &c.*

    Geographical and Astronomical Names, as, *continent, mountain, sea, sun, planet, &c.*

C. Abstract Nouns are names of Qualities, Powers, Feelings, Perceptions, Notions, Ideas, &c. as, *darkness, sorrow, heat, virtue, death, philosophy, poetry.*

EXERCISE V.

I. Write down { Deities, Men, Women, Countries, Cities, Mountains, Rivers } Proper Names of 1st Decl. ending in ( ); „ 2nd „ „ „ ( ); „ 3rd „ „ „ ( )

II. Write down ( ) Common Names, expressing

A. *a.* Persons having a right to command. *b.* Persons bound to obey. *c.* Persons engaged in any trade or profession. *d.* Persons of different ages. *e.* Kindred, &c.

B. *a:* Useful beasts. *b.* Noxious beasts. *c.* Harmless beasts. *d.* Useful birds. *e.* Singing birds. *f.* Birds of prey. *g.* Harmless birds. *h.* Useful fishes. *i.* Insects. *k.* Reptiles, &c.

C. *a.* Trees useful for their wood. *b.* Trees useful for their fruit. *c.* Fruits. *d.* Grains. *e.* Other useful plants. *f.* Flowers. *g.* Herbs, &c.

D. *a.* Natural Substances used in building a house. *b.* Natural Substances used in dress. *c.* Natural Substances used as food. *d.* Natural Substances used for ornament. *e.* The Elements, &c.

E. *a.* Human dwellings. *b.* Land and water carriages. *c.* Implements of agriculture. *d.* Implements of war. *e.* Implements of household use. *f.* Male clothing. *g.* Female clothing. *h.* Objects made of metal. *i.* Objects made of wood. *k.* Objects made of clay. *l.* Objects made of stone. *m.* Objects made of linen, or of wool. *n.* Objects made of skins. *o.* Objects in the school-room. *p.* Objects used in study. *q* Objects in a church, &c.

F. *a.* Parts of an animal. *b.* Parts of a horse. *c.* Parts of a cow. *d.* Parts of a sheep. *e.* Parts of the human body. *f.* Features of the human face. *g.* Organs of speaking and eating. *h.* Interior organs. *i.* Parts of a bird. *k.* Parts of a fish. *l.* Parts of an insect. *m.* Parts of a tree. *n.* Parts of the wheat-plant. *o.* Parts of a house. *p.* Parts of a ship. *q.* Parts of a city, &c.

G. *a.* Collections of men. *b.* Collections of animals.

H. *a.* Geographical Objects. *b.* Astronomical Objects.

III. Write down ( ) Abstract Names, expressing

a. Virtues. *b.* Vices. *c.* Faculties and Propensities of the human mind. *d.* Emotions. *e.* Parts of time. *f.* Casualties of life. *g.* Arts and Sciences. *h.* Governments. *i.* Occurrences of weather. *k.* Wants of Life. *l.* Good qualities of the body. *m.* Bad qualities of the body, &c.

N.B. The varieties of this exercise may be multiplied to any extent by the Master. The Genitive Case, Gender, and Declension of each word should be written down, and the words themselves occasionally declined.

EXERCISE VI.

A. Write down ( ) Adjectives
    a. of 3 Terminations, like bonus.
    b.   „   „   „   „   tener.
    c.   „   „   „   „   niger.
    d.   „   „   „   „   acer.
    e.   „ 2   „   „   „   tristis.
    f.   „ 1 Termination, like felix or ingens.
B. Compare these Adjectives.
C. Write down the Comparison of ( ) Adjectives
    a. compared like durus, brevis, audax.
    b.   „   „   pulcher.
    c.   „   „   celer.
    d.   „   „   facilis.
    e.   „   „   arduus.
    f. irregularly compared.

Question. — How are maledicus, strenuus, pius, compared? What Adjectives are compared like maledicus?

D. Write down the Comparison of ( ) Adverbs.
E.   „   „   „   „   „   sæpe, diu, penitus.
F. Compare 4 Adverbs having no Positive.
G.   „   3   „   „   „ Comparative.
H.   „   2   „   „   „ Superlative.

OBSERVATIONS.

Obs. II.—Adjectives express the qualities of persons and things; and this they may do in various respects: as of

    a. Size, as, *large, small, broad, narrow, &c.*
    b. Form, as, *round, square, angular, level, &c.*
    c. Colour, as, *white, black, green, blue, &c.*
    d. Situation, as, *near, distant, high, low, &c.*
    e. Material, as, *earthen, wooden, golden, woollen, &c.*
    f. Time, as, *old, young, ancient, new, &c.*
    g. Number, as, *one, two, three, few, many, &c.*
    h. Affection of Mind, as, *happy, sad, wise, foolish, &c.*
    i. Affection of Body, as, *strong, weak, healthy, &c.*
    k. Likeness, or Relation, as, *earthly, paternal, popular, sheepish, &c.*

N.B. Adjectives properly denoting an affection of body, size, form, &c. may (by the figure of speech called Metaphor) be applied to mind: as, *a narrow mind, a rough temper, a strong imagination, &c.*

Adjectives may express qualities perceived by

a. Touch, as, *rough, smooth, hard, soft, &c.*
b. Taste, as, *sweet, bitter, acid, insipid, &c.*
c. Smell, as, *fragrant, fetid, &c.*
d. Hearing, as, *loud, shrill, &c.*
e. Sight, as, *bright, dark, &c.*
f. Thought, as, *elegant, fit, pleasant, grievous, &c.*

N.B. Qualities perceived by thought are those which spring out of the relation between the object and the mind.

EXERCISE VII.

A. Write down ( ) Adjectives, expressing qualities *a.* of Size. *b.* of Situation. *c.* of Form. *d.* of Colour. *e.* of Material. *f.* of Time. *g.* of Mind. *h.* of Body. *i.* of Likeness, or Relation. *k.* perceived by Touch. *l.* perceived by Taste. *m.* perceived by Smell. *n.* perceived by Hearing. *o.* perceived by Sight. *p.* perceived by Thought.

B. Compare each of these Adjectives.

RULE AND OBSERVATIONS.

Rule I.—An Adjective agrees with its Substantive in Gender, Number, and Case : as, Rex bonus, *a good king.* Oppida capta, *captured towns.*

Obs. III.—For the purpose of agreement, Participles and Pronouns are to be regarded as Adjectives : except the Personal Pronouns, ego, tu, sui, which have the power of Substantives.

Obs. IV.—When the Adjective qualifies the Substantive without a Verb between them, it is called an *Attributive* or *Epithet.*

EXERCISE VIII.

A. *a.* Write down ( ) Epithets qualifying the Subst. ( )
of which let ( ) be of 3 Terminations, like bonus.

( )   „   „   „   „   niger.
( )   „   „   „   „   tener.
( )   „   „   „   „   acer.
( )   „   2   „   „   „   tristis.
( )   „   1 Termination, like felix or
                                           ingens.

   b. Which of these Epithets express Qualities of

       Size?   Situation?   Affection of Mind?
       Form?   Material?   Affection of Body?
       Colour?   Time?   Likeness or Relation?

     Which express Qualities perceived by

         Touch?   Hearing?
         Taste?   Sight?
         Smell?   Thought?

   c. Decline the Substantive ( ) with its Epithets.

B. *a.* Decline the ( ) Subst. ( ) with the Pron. hic.
   b.   „   „   „   „   „   „   „   is.
   c.   „   „   „   „   „   „   „   ille.
   d.   „   „   „   „   „   „   „   iste.
   e.   „   „   „   „   „   „   „   ipse.

and so through all the Adjective Pronouns, Numerals, &c.

C. *a.* Decline the ( ) Subst. ( ) with hic, and one other
                                            Epithet.
   b.   „   „   „   „   „   is,   „   „
   &c.   „   „   „   „   „   &c. „   „

D. *a.* Decline the ( ) Subst. ( ) with hic, and two other
                                            Epithets.
   b.   „   „   „   „   „   is,   „   „
   &c.   „   „   „   „   „   &c. „   „

     Conjunctions meaning *and, or, nor,* couple like Cases.

N.B. Any Substantives, or any portion of the Vocabulary, may be
appointed for this Exercise. It may be used also to teach the
difference of equivocal words. Thus the Substantives appointed
may be such as—clava, clavus, and clavis;—anous and anus;—
ora, hora, os (oris) and os (ossis); frons (frondis) and frons
(frontis);—mas and mare;—pila, pila, pilus and pilum;—plaga
and plaga;—aura, aurum, and auris;—arca, arx, and arcus;—
mala, malus, malum, and malum, &c. &c.

K

RULES and OBSERVATIONS.

Rule II.—When two Substantives, referred to the *same* thing, come together in the same clause, they are put in the same Case, and said to be in APPOSITION: as,

Philippus rex, *King Philip.*

Not. 1.—A Substantive may be in Apposition to a Pronoun, as,

Nos consules, *We the-Consuls.*

Not. 2.—A common instance of Apposition is that of the various names of one person, as,

Caius Julius Cæsar Octavianus Augustus.

Her Majesty Queen Victoria Alexandrina.

Rule III.—When two Substantives, referred to *different* things, come together in the same clause, one of them will be in the GENITIVE Case, with the sign *of:* as,

Ciceronis filius, *Son of Cicero,* or *Cicero's Son.*

Obs. V.—As an Epithet is an "*Attributive Adjective,*" so an Apposition is an "*Attributive Substantive,*" or "*Appositive;*" and a Genitive Subjectively governed by another Substantive is called its "*Attributive Genitive.*"

Rule IV.—The VOCATIVE is the Case of the person or thing spoken to, and is governed by an Interjection, expressed or understood: as,

Fili or O fili, *O son.*

EXERCISE IX.

A. *a.* Add Appositives to the Proper Names „ „ „ „;
and decline.

   b. Add Appositives with Epithet to the Proper Names „ „ „ „; and decline.

   c. Add Appositives with one or more Epithets each to the Common Nouns „ „ „ „; and decline.

d. Add an Appositive with one or more Epithets to the Personal Pronoun (   ); and decline them.

B. Add Substantives in the Genitive Case to the Substantives „ „ „ „; and decline.

C. *a.* Add Appositives, having one or more Epithets, and governing a Genitive Case, to the Substantives „ „ „ „ „ „ „; and decline.

b. Add an Appositive, having one or more Epithets, and governing a Genitive Case, to the Personal Pronoun (   ); and decline.

D. *a.* The Substantive (   ) or Pronoun (   ) being given, add to its Nominative Case any number of Appositives, with Genitive Cases, and Epithets.

b. The Substantive (   ) being given, add to its Vocative Case any number of Appositives, Genitive Cases, and Epithets.

E. *a.* Write down the Vocative Cases of the Substantives „ „ „ „ part with Interjections; part without an Interjection.

b. Write down the same Vocative Cases with one or more Epithets to each.

c. Add Appositives with Epithets, governing a Genitive Case with Epithets, to the same Vocative Cases.

Obs. VI.—Any Verb in a proper Mood is a *Finite* Verb. A Finite Verb is required to make a Sentence, or thought expressed in words. The Nominative Case (which is a Substantive, or that which has the force of a Substantive) is called the *Subject* of the Sentence, and the Verb is called the *Predicate;* and in the sentence Deus regnat, *God reigns,* Deus *(God)* is the Subject, and regnat *(reigns)* the Predicate. So Spiro *(I breathe)* is a Sentence; the Subject Ego being understood. But if you find any finite form of the Verb *sum* with a second Nominative Case after it, then that Verb is called the **Copula,** and the Nominative after it the *Predicate.* Thus in Deus est regnator, *God is ruler;* nos sumus servi, *we are servants:* Deus *(God)* and nos *(we)* are the *Subjects;* est and sumus the *Copulas;* regnator *(ruler)* and servi *(servants)* the *Predicates.* A Verb which governs an Accusative Case of that on which it acts is called a *Transitive* Verb; and the Accusative is called the *Nearer Object;* as, Deus regit mundum, *God rules the world;* where mundum is *Nearer Object* of regit. A Verb which cannot govern a Nearer Object is called an *Intransitive* or *Neuter* Verb, and cannot be used personally in the Passive Voice, as ambulo, *I walk,* If the Verb has two objects, the other is called the *Remoter Object,* and this is generally in the Dative Case: as, Pater librum filio dat, *the father gives the book to the son;* where librum is the Nearer, filio the Remoter, Object of the Verb dat.

EXERCISE X.

Write down

A. *a.* ( ) Transitive Verbs Act. of 1st Conjug.
   b. ( )   ,,   ,,   ,,   ,, 2nd   ,,
   c. ( )   ,,   ,,   ,,   ,, 3rd   ,,
   d. ( )   ,,   ,,   ,,   ,, 4th   ,,
B. *a.* ( ) Transitive Verbs Deponent of 1st Conjug.
   b. ( )   ,,   ,,   ,,   ,,   ,, 2nd   ,,
   c. ( )   ,,   ,,   ,,   ,,   ,, 3rd   ,,
   d. ( )   ,,   ,,   ,,   ,,   ,, 4th   ,,
C. *a.* ( ) Neuter Verbs Active of 1st Conjug.
   b. ( )   ,,   ,,   ,,   ,, 2nd   ,,
   c. ( )   ,,   ,,   ,,   ,, 3rd   ,,
   d. ( )   ,,   ,,   ,,   ,, 4th   ,,
D. *a.* ( ) Neuter Verbs Deponent of 1st Conjug.
   b. ( )   ,,   ,,   ,,   ,, 2nd   ,,
   c. ( )   ,,   ,,   ,,   ,, 3rd   ,,
   d. ( )   ,,   ,,   ,,   ,, 4th   ,,

N.B. *Let each Verb be conjugated, and let the Master require the Latin for any English form of a Verb, as,* we should have complained, be ye judged; *and the English for any Latin form, as,* paravero, partiti erant.

RULE and OBSERVATIONS.

Rule V.—A Finite Verb agrees with its Nominative Case in Number and Person: as, Deus regnat, *God reigns;* nos moriemur, *we shall die.*

Obs. VII.—The Nominative, when a Pronoun, is generally omitted: as, moriemur, *we shall die.*

Obs. VIII.—The Nominatives *men* and *things* are often understood from Epithets: as, multi dixerant, *many men had said;* omnia mutantur, *all things are changed.*

EXERCISE XI.

A. Write down ( ) suitable Nominatives, with an Epithet to each, agreeing with the Finite Verb ( ).
  N.B. Let the Declensions be varied.

B. Write down ( ) suitable Finite Verbs, agreeing with the Nominative ( ): of which Verbs ( ) shall be Active, ( ) Passive, ( ) Deponent, ( ) of 1st Conjug. ( ) of 2nd, &c. &c.: ( ) in the Indicative Mood, ( ) in the Conjunctive, ( ) in the Imperative: and each (if possible) in a different Tense.

C. Make ( ) Sentences, each of two words, from Sections ( ) of the Vocabulary.

RULE and OBSERVATION.

Rule VI.—Copulative Verbs of any Mood have the same Case after as before them; as, Socrates erat philosophus, *Socrates was a philosopher;* nos fiemus docti, *we shall become learned.*

Obs. IX.—Copulative Verbs are so called, because, like the Copula sum *(I am),* which is the principal of them, they connect the Subject and a *distinct* Predicate, which may be a Substantive or an Adjective. If a Substantive, it agrees with the Subject in the same manner as an Appositive: if an Adjective, in the same manner as an Epithet. The chief of these Verbs,

L

besides sum, are fio, *I become* or *am made*, nascor, *I am born*, videor, *I seem*, and Passives of *making, naming, declaring, choosing, thinking, finding, showing, &c.* ; as,

efficior
creor } *I am made.*

appellor
vocor } *I am called.*

nominor
nuncupor } *I am named.*

dicor
feror
narror } *I am said.*

declaror
renuntior } *I am declared.*

eligor, *I am chosen.*

existimor
putor } *I am thought.*

credor
habeor } *I am supposed.*

invenior
reperior } *I am found.*

noscor
cognoscor } *I am known.*

agnoscor, *I am acknow- ledged.*

EXERCISE XII.

A. Construct ( ) Sentences with the Substantive ( ), the Copulative Verb sum in various Moods and Tenses, and
    (a) a Predicate Substantive.
    (b) a Predicate Adjective.

B. Construct ( ) Sentences with the Substantive ( ), the Copulative Verb ( ) in various Moods and Tenses, and
    (a) a Predicate Substantive.
    (b) a Predicate Adjective.

C. Construct ( ) Sentences with the Copulative Verbs sum, fio, &c. and the Substantives and Adjectives - - - - - -, varying the Verbs, Moods, Tenses, Declensions, &c.

N.B. The principle of the foregoing Exercises may easily be carried on to the remaining elementary rules of Latin Syntax: as Government of Cases by Prepositions, the Accusative of the Nearer Object, the Dative of the Remoter Object, the Genitive Partitive and Objective, the Ablative of Circumstance, &c. &c. See 'the Child's Latin Primer,' and the Elementary Latin Grammar.

FINIS.

PRINTED BY JOHN DAVIES, SHREWSBURY.

Lightning Source UK Ltd.
Milton Keynes UK
UKHW020919150822
407319UK00007B/1449